Blogging <u>IS</u> A Real Job!

…and it pays well, too!

F. Nasim

ISBN: 9798393904692

DEDICATION

I dedicate this book to all those in the world who choose to uplift, support, inspire and encourage others to grow into their best selves.

May we know these people, and may we become these people.

Thank you to the two little humans who, by simply being their wonderful selves, remind me daily to always work harder and do better.

CONTENTS

1
Introduction

My story

I was in my final year of my undergraduate degree at university, a few months shy of my final exams and very likely in dire need of finishing my dissertation, when I started my food blog, Fatima Cooks.

I was procrastinating from my work, big time. Again.

I'd just taught myself how to cook and had become very passionate about sharing it with the world. After struggling to learn Pakistani cooking myself using the very few resources the online world had to offer at that time, I was frustrated - but I also realised there was a gap in the market for someone like me. This realisation became the catalyst that led me to create a website sharing my collection of traditional Pakistani recipes that had been meticulously taste-tested, easy to follow, detailed and, of course, delicious.

It wasn't my first blog, no (it wasn't my last, either!) I had started a health and fitness blog just one year earlier but it very quickly stalled and failed to build a readership beyond my 3,000 Instagram followers at the time. I wasn't passionate or knowledgeable enough about it, nor did I invest any time into learning about how best to run a blog.

'Fatima Cooks' was different. I went into it with clearer, more ambitious intent, ready to learn the ins and outs of blogging.

I didn't start out making any money. My goal was to eventually figure out how to make income from my blog some day, but I definitely underestimated the potential of the blogging world. 'If I can ONE DAY start making £1000 a month from this, I'll be absolutely content,' I told myself determinedly.

I dove into my blog with the right work ethic and discipline, but less than a year into my venture, I was hit by a number of significant life changes: my first year teaching at a high school, my first pregnancy, a hyperemesis one at that, followed by the full-blown postpartum experience of a newborn who seemed allergic to sleep, and a traumatic death in our immediate family - just a short list of all the whammies of that year. It all meant I had to abandon the blog for two years. I left it running, so it was still on the internet, but I stopped monitoring it, updating it or responding to comments on it. At this stage, I had already published around 40-50 posts.

Unbeknownst to me, during those two years, my blog gained a tonne of traction, steadily growing into a very popular source for those looking for Pakistani recipes. My recipes began showing up on the first page of Google, were shared on various other websites and I gained many loyal, returning visitors who had grown to enjoy my content. Traffic ramped up.

When I eventually did find my way back to my blog, I realised I could monetise my traffic immediately by applying to a higher-paying display ad network. When I did, my first monthly payment - for something I hadn't touched in two years - was for £900.

It was never the same after that.

I don't like dwelling on regrets, but I do wonder what would have happened if I had known my blog would grow into a full-time income organically. If I had prioritised my blog or believed it could earn me more money than I had envisaged, I likely wouldn't have abandoned it the way I had, and I would have started earning more income much earlier than I did.

'Fatima Cooks' surpassed my original goal of £1000/month in 2019, and in 2020 began pulling in an income which was greater than my old teaching job. All that from a cute little blog started by someone who had no training or experience with web design and tech, who had just taken a bunch of pictures on her iPhone 3GS, but had a passion for sharing her best recipes.

As I mentioned earlier, 'Fatima Cooks' hasn't been my only blog, it's just been my most profitable and longest-standing one (so far). My first health and fitness blog of 2014 was a lost cause - I don't even remember the name of it anymore. In 2017, I started an e-commerce fashion website which I ran for 2 years - it was an incredibly successful venture but eventually the very active nature of selling physical products, dealing with customers, stockists and postage began to wear on me to the extent that I began to dread my work. I shut it down in 2019 as soon as I realised the huge potential of passive income from 'Fatima Cooks'. In 2021, I started a blog about teaching children the Urdu language called 'My Zuban'. It's currently up and running, bringing in a small but consistent income from digital product sales and I'm incredibly excited about the potential it holds too. This year I've started two new blogs - one, a joint venture with my husband about garment production, and two, a blog in ode to this book: a blog about... blogging (you can check it out at FNasim.com, although at the time of publishing this book, it's very much in its infancy).

Throughout this book, I will refer mostly to my food and language blogs because they are the two I've learnt the most lessons from and are most relevant to you.

I truly feel that blogging is one of the best kept secrets of the passive income world. It's something that has absolutely transformed my life and allowed me to earn potentially more than I ever would have had I gone back to work after children, whilst working fewer hours in a week than I can count on my fingers.

Blogging often gets overlooked and people favour creating social media or YouTube content - both of which, mind you, are also fantastic, viable ways to make money. But I love blogging for its evergreen nature, its slower pace and its consistency in favouring solid, good content over whatever is trending and viral at the moment.

Starting a blog is not hard or complicated - it's just a simple cocktail of finding the right niche, learning how to write in a Google-friendly format, strategising efficiently and having patience during the initial process. I can understand that from a distance, it feels difficult, out of reach or something that can only be done by a professional. **I promise you, this is not true.**

Having a reliable source of passive or semi-passive income is not only empowering, it is life changing. You gain back so many hours of your life - hours you can spend doing the things you love, spending time with your loved ones, working on other projects dear to you. And the hours you do spend working? You spend them working for yourself, writing about a topic you enjoy and are good at, helping others and serving a community at large. I repeat what I said earlier: I think online blogging is one of the best kept secrets of the world.

Imagine waking up one day in one year's time, checking your accounts and knowing you've made £100, £200, £300 or more yesterday without having done more than a few hours' work this week.

How does that make you feel?

Now imagine getting that feeling every day. Even on weekends. Even on bank holidays. Even on days and weeks you haven't worked a single minute.

Every single day.

It's liberating. It's invigorating.

And I'm here to tell you it's 100% attainable. It's not some sort of fantasy reserved only for those with a degree in English or website design. It's not an elusive thing only for some and not all. You CAN start a successful, profitable blog. Blogging IS a viable career, it IS a real job! Blogging has the potential to earn you a 5-, 6- or even 7-figure income - there is no ceiling! And I'll show you how to start in this book.

Glad to have you on this journey!

Who this book is for

If you want to get into blogging but are not quite sure what it entails, what it could do for you or how to start, I've written this book for you.

If you feel daunted and overwhelmed at the steps you need to take to have a successful, profitable blog, but know it's something you want for yourself, I've written this book for you.

If you are a beginner with minimal knowledge about blogging jargon, online technicalities, and all the fancy search engine science, I've written this book for you.

My approach is to break it all down for you step by step, just how I would have liked it to have been laid out for me when I first started.

I will dispel those nasty myths that you have to spend hundreds or thousands of pounds on branding, web design or equipment before starting up (in fact, I believe you **shouldn't** do that, period).

Blogging is not complicated. It is just unfamiliar territory at first, and that too just for a short while. If you're willing to get stuck in and learn what you need to build something amazing, then this book is for you.

How to use this book

This book has been written to guide you chronologically through your blogging journey.

Where relevant, a task is included for you to reflect on the knowledge you've learnt and to help you hone in on your thoughts and ideas. Space has been provided for you to write notes within this book, or you can complete the tasks in a separate notebook.

Every effort has been made to break down the blogging jargon as much as possible throughout the book, however, I have also included a glossary at the end of the book to help you with these terms.

2
Why Blog?

Blogging in its most simple definition is a regularly updated website run by either an individual or a small company who shares their experiences, insights or information about a certain topic. It more often than not has a more informal, sociable and conversational voice. You feel like there's a person at the other end of the post, not a robot or a lifeless academic/salesperson.

Blogging has seen a bit of an uptick over the last few years, particularly since the pandemic in 2020, when people sought out novel ways to make money from home. The pandemic era was definitely pivotal for me too - it's when my blog tipped over into full-time income territory and I know it did for many others too.

But blogging isn't actually novel - it's been around in some form or another since the inception of the home computer system. Evidence suggests the first ever blog was created in 1994! People just love to write and share information! But the world of blogging has become much more sophisticated and, quite frankly, incredibly more profitable than ever before. I genuinely believe it's one of the most underrated sources of income, especially for an introvert like me who finds it very empowering hiding behind a screen to make a living.

But what makes blogging so good? What makes it stand out from other ways of making money from home, like opening up a social media account, a YouTube or a business selling products?

We all love a bit (or a lot!) of passive income

Passive income is a bit of a buzzword nowadays. Everyone wants passive income and everyone wants to learn how to make it. But not everyone knows how to.

The truth about passive income is… it doesn't actually start out passive. In fact, passive income requires a lot of upfront work. But once that work is done, your foundation is set up and it begins to generate income, you can sit back and enjoy your hard work with only a fraction of the effort you put into it at the start.

Once you've set up your blog and begin to generate enough traffic (a fancy word for readers) to be able to make some money , you'll begin to earn passive income, whether you continue to work on your blog or not. (I will go into more detail about how to make money from your blog in chapter 12.) Since blogging requires upkeep, maintenance, and in most cases, creating some new content to keep your readers interested, I would suggest semi-passive is a more accurate word. However, the time spent doing all those things can be as much or as little as you'd like it to be.

In my case, I set up my food blog and once I began to earn a sizable amount of income passively, I was able to dip in and out of spending time on the blog as and when my life situation allowed me. I spent the majority of 2021 completely away from my food blog tending to my newborn son and working on my language blog, uploading just one new post between January and November - but I still made a full-time income from it. In fact, my blog traffic grew by 20% that year.

How could I do that? Because I had already done the front-end work! I had built a blog that brought in enough traffic from search engines and other sources and which did not rely on me having to be constantly working. **THAT is the power of passive income.** I now create new content to help me grow my income, but if I were to ever step away from my food blog for a large period of time again like I did in 2021, **my income would largely remain the same**.

Just imagine that for a moment. Imagine being able to earn a good chunk of money every month without doing ANYTHING - simply being paid for what you did a few months or years ago? Imagine the amount of freedom, peace of mind and happiness that would give you.

Blogs don't need you to be 'active' all the time

If the thought of having a constant 'presence' sounds exhausting, introverts, you can breathe a sigh of relief!

Unlike social media, where today's algorithms mean you need to be posting very often for people to see and remember you, blogs don't need that sort of constant TLC. Once your blog is ranking on search engines and driving traffic, it will continue to bring the traffic in without you needing to intervene. Once your posts begin to show up in the top positions for a search query, it will show up every time someone searches for it on Google - whether you do anything or not.

This is a great benefit of running an online blog because the risk of social media burnout is very real, especially with the constantly shifting algorithms and the broad move towards a more video-centric, quantity-over-quality model.

Blogs are evergreen. Social media platforms are not.

I remember when Facebook first came on the block - it launched in 2004 and I became aware of it in 2008 as a young girl in high school, making my first account on it from the PC in my living room. I then watched it transform before my eyes into a near-monopoly over the internet, becoming everyone's preferred way to communicate and share information. In 2010, Instagram came onto the scene and slowly began to chip away at Facebook's members base. In recent times, Tiktok has been taking over what sometimes feels like life as we know it. Facebook? Facebook now has a reputation as being 'uncool' and 'dated'. In fact, the majority of its users are now in their 40's and 50's. For young adults, YouTube, TikTok, Instagram and Snapchat stand out as their social media of choice.

What am I getting at with all this?

Social media is not a permanent, infinitely existing platform and is constantly evolving - the adage of 'out with the old, in with the new' comes to mind. New platforms come, with their new and fresh outlook, entice new members in and go on to have a lifespan of a few years - until another new social media platform comes to rule them all again. We saw it happen to MySpace, Tumblr, Facebook - it's a cycle that is inevitable and unavoidable.

Creating a website, however? This is not something that will ever die down. It is not subject to the life cycle of social networks in the same way - websites are the basis of internet life as we know it and they are here to stay.

This is certainly not to write off social media networks. Social media holds an undeniably huge amount of influence and it's powerful to leverage that for your blog. But my advice is to always have your 'home base' as your blog, not your social media.

Your work is on your terms

I love blogging, period. But this reason here really takes the cake for me - that I only work for myself. I answer to myself.

Any deadlines I need to reach are imposed on by myself. I get to choose my layout, colour palette and design choices. What I choose to write or not write, what strategies I implement and how much time I spend on my blog - these are all my choices.

Some people will do really well with this sort of independent framework. Personally, it's the only way I can function and for me, there's nothing quite like that kind of mental freedom.

Blogger skills are VALUABLE

One of the best pieces of career advice I've ever received was from a lady in her 60s who did not look like the poster-image of a career woman. She sat me down in her house as she was cooking a feast of Pakistani food for me dressed in traditional attire, speaking in Urdu to me. She had under her belt a variety of degrees, qualifications and courses, including training in immigration and law, property planning permission, accounting, business management, commercial property, banking, languages and seamstressing.

Her golden, life changing advice? **Never outsource a task that you will need on the regular - invest in learning it.** Not only will it save you money, time and hassle in the long run, you'll do it better justice doing it how you like it. My approach to life, not just blogging, was impacted forever (thank you, Aunty!) Throughout this book, you'll see I'm a big advocate for not spending excessive money on things people may tell you to invest in otherwise. I am, however, big on investing time and/or money in learning valuable skills from reputable sources to excel at blogging and quicken your road to success.

As your blog grows, you may eventually choose to outsource some of your tasks, and that's absolutely fine (and in fact, necessary to eventually scale your blog). I still advocate for learning those skills anyway, so that you're self-sufficient and can operate your blog efficiently by yourself.

To be a successful blogger, the skills you will learn and repeatedly apply are not only useful for you, but are also transferrable and in very high demand. If you're in any other line of work or business, these skills will benefit you tremendously. You can offer some of these as services to others too - in fact, I've seen many bloggers provide these skills on a freelance basis to tide them over until their blog begins to pull in a full-time income. Such skills may include:

- Copywriting and editing.
- Search engine optimisation.

- Keyword research.
- Photography.
- Email marketing.
- Social media management/marketing.
- Proofreading.
- Accounting tasks.

Please note: I'm not against outsourcing aspects of your blog work in the early days, but I am partial towards only doing so when you can justify the expense from your profits.

A successful blog is also an asset that can be sold. A ballpark figure for a blog's selling value is 36x its average monthly income - so if your blog is generating £2,000/month, you could consider selling it for £72,000!

SUMMARY

Starting a blog is a much more passive way of making money than many people realise. Blogs are a stable, evergreen platform as opposed to the ever-changing world of social media. Therefore, blogs and websites are not subject to the volatility of algorithms and social network life cycles, and you can do the work on your own terms. The skills you will pick up while learning how to blog are

highly valuable and sought after, and have the potential of opening up other avenues of work too.

3

Is Blogging Right For You?

Many come into the arena of blogging with a no-holds-barred approach, ready to take on everything and are prepared to Do All The Things with confidence. Some, however, will question whether it's the right path for them. That's very normal and in fact, a very smart thing to do! It's definitely wise to consider what your goals are, what running a successful blog entails and whether it aligns with what you want and are capable of.

One thing that I'd like you to really embrace as you read this book is that almost **anyone can run a successful blog if they are willing to learn how**. It's certainly a learning curve with trial and error involved, but thousands of others have done it and you can too. Many people have convinced themselves they are not cut out for blogging because they aren't talented or skilled enough. This just isn't true and is a self sabotaging, limiting belief - something I'll discuss in the next chapter.

Figuring out your income goals

Everyone's income goals for blogging may look different. Setting goals is a good starting point because it sets up your expectations from the get-go. Your goals may be anything, including:

- To have a supplemental income that helps you pay the bills or cushion your savings.
- To make a full-time income.
- To carve a space in your industry and become an authority figure in your niche.
- To get your small business noticed by more people.

Some people will want to blog because:

- They want to make more money.
- They want to make money passively.
- They want to replace or reduce hours at their day job.
- They want to share a passion with the world.
- They have a small business and it makes sense to blog about it.

Or all of the above!

All of these goals are very much achievable as a blogger

and this book will detail how to get started with it.

There are many bloggers in the industry who make a 5-, 6-, 7- and even 8-figure income from blogging. A quick Google search for 'top earning blogs last year' will show some mind blowing figures. But even if you don't eye up the highest earners in the industry, here are some income stats based on a survey[1] of 4000+ bloggers reporting their monthly earnings:

- Less than $10/month: 30%
- $10-$99: 24%
- $100-$499: 17%
- $500-$999: 6%
- $1000-$2499: 7%
- $2500-$4999: 3%
- $5000-$14999: 3%
- $15000+: 10%

So according to this survey, 29% of bloggers are earning $500 or more monthly and 23% of bloggers are earning $1000 or more a month. What could possibly be the difference between these ranges? Direction, strategy, knowledge and experience. I'll be talking about all of these further on to help you increase the likelihood of you making a better income from your blog quicker.

TASK: Think about what kind of income goals you'd like to achieve through your blog. Have a look at the statistics I've shared in this section and consider how much you'd like to aim for in 2, 5 and 10 years' time. 'Chapter 4: Overcoming Mental Barriers' may also help you with this if you're feeling stuck or scared of aiming too high.

Basic skills you need to run a successful blog

While I do say anyone can start a blog, there are certain skills that make running a successful blog more likely. You don't necessarily need to have these skills before you start - some of these skills will be fostered as you write content and grow - but these are good points to consider before deciding whether you want to dive into blogging.

A genuine passion or expertise in an area

This is a non-negotiable. In order for blogging to work for you, you'll have to create a lot of content consistently over a long period of time. And quite frankly, if you aren't passionate or at the very least knowledgeable about your chosen area, that's a very difficult job to commit to. At best, you'll find the job painstakingly boring and at worst, you'll get so underwhelmed you'll quit. So only get into this if you know you love what you're writing about. As the saying goes, if you do what you love, you'll never work a day in your life.

English writing skills

The most basic skill, the very pinnacle of blogging - you should be able to write long-form content and do it with good command of the English language. Most blog posts should be a minimum of 1000 words (but 2000-3000 is a better range), so being a good writer will go a long way for you in keeping readers on board and establishing yourself as an intelligent blogger.

Writing is a skill that develops with practice, so if you aren't confident in your abilities, don't write blogging off (pun intended) just yet. However, if you're less of a writer and more of a speaker, then maybe you should consider whether a different avenue (such as YouTube) would be better for you.

A basic grasp of the technology

By this I don't mean knowing how to code or getting into the HTML to rewrite your blog layout. If you've ever turned on a laptop, sent an email, attached a file to an email, searched for something on Google or used an app to edit a photo, I am 99.9% sure you have more than enough of a grasp over technical things to learn how to blog.

Some of the 'scarier' tasks such as setting up the layout of your blog will be a one-and-done thing, and other aspects which you'll be doing more regularly are not very challenging to learn. You'll be fine, I promise.

Willingness to be patient and focused

Blogging is NOT an overnight ticket to money and success. I like to think of it as a fruit tree - anyone who has any experience with gardening will know that most fruit trees don't actually bear any fruit the first year, even with all the tender love, care and expensive fertiliser in the world. Some don't even bear fruit the second year. But when they eventually do bear fruit, the tree continues to grow and get stronger every year.

I'm very transparent about the fact that blogging is unlikely to bring you a sizable income for likely 12-18 months. There are ways to accelerate that timeline, but the truth is it takes around that much time to build an audience for most people. Getting through that initial slog can be TOUGH. We're all busy; many of us have day jobs, children and other commitments which can make dedicating time to something that requires a lot of upfront work and isn't generating money HARD. So having focus and discipline is a very important element in blogging in the early days - eyes on the prize!

This is alas a short list - but it goes to show that the bar to start a blog is actually pretty low, and actually, the biggest determinant of running a profitable, successful blog is more to do with mindset and consistency than anything else!

SUMMARY

Blogging can be for anyone and everyone, regardless of how vast your goals may be - but having these qualities will make it a better fit for some more than others. You don't need to have been in the gifted and talented cohort at school, have a fancy qualification or have insider contacts in Google in order to start a successful blog. Nonetheless, it's good to have the 'is this right for me?' conversation with yourself before committing, as you likely will not see the fruits of your labours for some time.

4

Overcoming Mental Barriers

Before we start any new project, it's very natural to feel overwhelmed by thoughts pulling and pushing us in different directions.

'It won't work, it's too hard.'
'I feel really ready for this.'
'Someone has already done this before, I don't have a chance.'
'I have so many unique perspectives and so much information to share.'
'No one is interested in what I have to say.'
'I want to leave a mark in my industry and I think I can do it.'

It can feel very burdonsome sifting through all those thoughts!

Mindset plays a huge role in how we approach new projects and what we believe we can achieve. When we have a limiting mindset, we put a glass ceiling over our heads, inadvertently self sabotaging our potential. I'm going to spend some time breaking down these mindsets and how they can impact your blogging aspirations.

Scarcity mindset

Scarcity mindset, also known as a mindset of lack, is a fixed mindset in which we believe resources and money are **limited, finite and inaccessible to us**. It makes us hold onto whatever resources and money we may have, scared to lose or share it and unwilling to do anything which may jeopardise it. It makes people fearful, anxious, risk averse, selfish and pessimistic.

Scarcity mindset often finds its way into our cognitive reasoning after repeated bad experiences, failures, or even during our childhood if we witnessed scarcity growing up. Mindset is contagious - if we spend time with partners, friends or anyone with a scarcity mindset, it can rub off on us. Fear is a very powerful emotion and holds us back considerably from getting ahead in our lives, relationships and careers.

Scarcity mindset is around us everywhere. It is the most predominant mindset that people harbour - although some will have a stronger scarcity mindset than others.

It's there when someone begrudgingly accepts their reality as being fixed and unchangeable, because change is hard and a pleasant reality is only for the lucky ones.

It's there whenever someone forgoes their dream business because they're scared of investing time and resources on it when there's a chance it may fail.

It's there when someone doesn't share their methods and ways to succeed at something because they don't want anyone to outshine them.

It's there when someone doesn't invest in their future selves because the future is too far away and they just want to focus on making it through today.

It's there when someone shies away from trying something new because they're not immediately good at it and that's something they absolutely cannot bear.

It's there when someone views a failure as a personal insult and never goes down that path again.

It's there when someone doesn't support or uplift another person doing well because they're scared of their success - because it means there won't ever be room for them to be successful.

Do any of these thoughts remind you of someone or sound... familiar?

When we tell ourselves *'I'll start my blog when I'm older, wiser, richer, freer, when I've done that course or once I feel ready'*, it comes from a scarcity mindset.

Scarcity mindset is finding excuses to not do something bigger and better because we're scared. Scared of failing, scared of not being noticed, scared of wasting time and resources, scared of never making it, and so on.

Scarcity mindset is self-sabotage. And it's the number one reason why most people won't ever break the cycle and do anything extraordinary in their careers or personal finance.

Abundance mindset

An abundance mindset is the opposite of a scarcity mindset. It believes there are **infinite, unlimited resources out there and if we do not have them, we can find ways to access them.**

An abundance mindset fosters empowerment, a go-getter attitude, willingness to uplift and support others, and is optimistic.

An abundance mindset is not the predominant mindset most people have. But I can guarantee you, when you meet people with this mindset, they will inspire, uplift and empower you. I'm sure we all have come across at least one person in our lives like this. They light up rooms and inspire change in others.

When someone in an unpleasant circumstance takes charge of their situation and makes change, even if that change is uncomfortable or hard, that's an abundance mindset.

When somebody chooses to invest time and resources on their dreams, that's an abundance mindset.

When somebody happily shares their wins, their wisdoms and experiences because they want everyone to win and they know they don't lose out when someone else wins, that's an abundance mindset.

When someone chooses to invest in their future because they know they are worth investing in, that's an abundance mindset.

When someone is willing to try something new and learn new skills, even though they may not be good at it at first, because they know everyone has to start somewhere, that's an abundance mindset.

When someone doesn't take failures personally and uses their mistakes as an opportunity to learn and grow, that's an abundance mindset.

When someone open-heartedly supports and uplifts others who are doing well because they are genuinely happy for their wins and knows it has no negative impact on their own wins or losses, that's an abundance mindset.

When you start a new blog from scratch, it can be scary because you have to learn a lot of new skills, invest time and effort into it, and then be patient with the results. But if you foster an abundance mindset, you'll be able to see the bigger picture - that this is an investment in your future, a testimony to the fact that you believe in your skills and believe you are worthy of pursuing and attaining your goals.

Reframing your thoughts to cultivate this sort of a mindset can be very difficult if you have a scarcity mindset. For some, it can feel uncomfortable facing those fearful thoughts, looking them in the eye and saying 'nope, not this time' - but it's also one of the most liberating, freeing things you will ever do for yourself.

The great thing about a scarcity mindset is that it's not fixed for life, and you CAN retrain your brain to think differently. It involves stopping negative, scarce thoughts in their tracks and replacing them with positive affirmations and beliefs. It initially won't come naturally, especially if you've been thinking from a place of scarcity for a long time. But this is an integral part of self-growth and getting ahead in life more generally, not just in terms of blogging.

TASK: Write down the first three mindset barriers or reservations that come to mind about you starting a blog.

Once you've got those down, switch roles and imagine you are reading these reservations written by an intelligent, competent and resourceful individual who you know is 100% capable of smashing it. How would you respond to them to calm their fears? Write down your responses underneath in a different colour.

Remember, *you are an intelligent, competent and resourceful individual.* But until you realise it, you won't be able to hone in on your abilities and skills.

I did this very task for myself before I started to write this book. Here's what was on my paper.

I'm scared no one will read my book.

I have so much value and experience to share with the world. People will read my book and benefit from it. If not as many people read it as I would like, then I can find ways to get my book to reach more people.

I don't know how to handle the logistics of writing, proofreading, marketing and publishing a book, and I feel overwhelmed.

I can learn. Others have done this before me, so I can learn from their experiences and do it too. I have taught myself many new skills in the past, and this will be no different. One foot in front of the other and I'll get there.

I'm scared it won't do well and that would look bad on me.

If I put thought, effort and time into my book, people will find value in it and it will do well. And even if it doesn't do as well as I like, it is not a moral failing and not a reflection of how good I am as a person.

Why do some blogs fail?

'All this talk about a positive, abundant mindset is all well and good, but if it was so easy, everyone would be doing it.' I hear some cry.

There are a variety of different reasons why people start out their blogs starry-eyed and optimistic and then never see their efforts come to fruition.

Let me make this clear: blogs have HUGE potential to grow and become a source of income for you, but **not every blog attains that**. It's a two-part equation - **you have to have the right mindset AND do the work properly**. Remember, all issues can be tackled and there is a solution to every problem. That's why having the right mindset is so important - when we understand that we can get things moving in the right direction when things aren't going well, we're more inclined to believe in ourselves and actually take those steps, instead of throwing in the towel and calling foul play.

Let's take a look at a few common reasons why some bloggers aren't successful and what can be done to tackle those issues.

They give up on their blog or strategy too early

Blog growth takes TIME. Motivation can dip, especially when you're pouring hard work into something that isn't bringing in any money.

If you have read about other people's blog journeys and stories, you may find some people talking about how they grew their blog into a profitable business within months - in fact, there is an abundance of bloggers online claiming it took them 6 months or less to begin earning a few thousand pounds or more a month. And it can be disheartening not seeing those results for yourself.

Whilst I don't question the authenticity of their claims, I do have other questions:

- Did they hire content writers, SEO experts or outsource any of their services to grow their blog quicker?

- Did they already have a substantial readership from another platform, such as email lists or social media, which helped them drive traffic?

- Was it their first blog, or did they have experience and expertise from creating previous blogs?

- Were they targeting a very specialised niche that was low competition and high traffic?

- What was the breakdown of their income? Was their income primarily from selling products or services, display ads or affiliate marketing?

These factors can all play a role in bringing in revenue quicker than the average blogger. When these claims are backed with statistics and a breakdown of how they did it, I love the opportunity to learn from their experiences, as opposed to finding their success a reason to feel despondent at my own progress.

Now, a more realistic perspective. Research from a survey[1] shows it takes on average 20 months to start making money with blogging. This length of time can be attributed to the learning curve new bloggers will go through before figuring out what works for them. However, **27% of bloggers say they do make some money within 6 months of starting and 38%**

of those who stay on by the 2 year mark are able to make a full-time income from it. This same study shows a **correlation between the age of the blog and the income made.**

These statistics are reassurance that staying on board for the long term is key.

And remember, if you have the right knowledge, strategy and direction, you can begin to earn money quicker than these averages. Money from display ads can take time to begin rolling in, so you can diversify your streams of income to include affiliate marketing, working with brands and/or selling products/services, so you don't have to wait a very long time to begin pulling in at least enough money to cover costs. But the key thing to remember is it will take time for things to kick in.

They don't have a strategy

Strategising your blog work is a very important part of growing your business to bring in more than a few pennies here and there.

Strategy is a word that makes some people feel overwhelmed, but it really doesn't have to be complicated. A strategy is just a road map to how you're going to achieve your goals and the steps you are going to take to achieve what you've set out. **A simple, well-researched strategy executed consistently is enough to steer things in the right direction.**

Here's an example of a very simple strategy that, when executed properly, will lead to good growth:

- Targeting low competition, medium search volume keywords for posts (I'll be going into what competition and volume means in chapter 6).

- Doing competitor research before writing posts to ensure your post is the most comprehensive, well-written post for your chosen keyword.

- Posting on your blog 6-8x a month in the first few months, then bringing the quantity down to 3-4x a month once the blog reaches 50 posts.

- Collecting emails for a weekly email newsletter which provides value to readers and also redirects them to content from your blog, growing loyalty and gaining returning visitors.

- Opening and actively running a Pinterest account through which to gain readership.

This plan is simple and to the point. For the sake of transparency, this is just the skeleton of a good, thorough strategy and ideally, there will need to be more details fleshed out (e.g., what content to post on social media, content for the email newsletters, etc.) It doesn't have to be incredibly fancy or complicated - but it does need to be there.

Going into any business, blogging or not, without a plan is a terribly ineffective way to go about things. It's like poking around in the mud without a metal detector hoping to find gold.

They aren't optimised for search engines

The truth is, your blog needs to be optimised for search engines in order to have consistent growth and traffic. Social media traffic will often come in waves and is subject to unpredictable algorithms, but search engine traffic is reliable and the key to growing your blog into a profitable business. Learning about and implementing search engine optimisation techniques should be an essential part of your job blogging.

Search engine optimisation isn't just writing good quality content (although that is a very big element of it!) Using heading tags correctly, adding descriptions to your images, ensuring your blog isn't slow, making sure you've targeted the keywords correctly - these all are important tweaks which make a huge difference to how search engines can scan and therefore rank your blog. You can have the greatest, top quality posts but if your posts are not optimised for search engines, it will be an uphill battle getting your blog the traffic it deserves.

While search engine optimisation is a vast topic and possibly deserves a book of its own, I share the most important ways to use SEO practices on your blog throughout this book.

The posts are not of a sound standard

The importance of this is paramount for success - your content needs to be high quality in order to stand a chance. The market today is saturated with blogs and websites - providing quality and value is the only way you can cut through the noise and impress your audience enough to keep them coming back for more.

The issue I see predominantly is people thinking their work isn't good enough because it isn't a 10/10 masterpiece. This crippling desire for perfection stops them from even trying their hand at blogging, even if they have so much to offer. At the other end of the spectrum however, are people who think they can upload content that is probably a 4/10 with poor grammar and structure, too many filler words that add little value and are irritatingly click-baity. In some niches, it may be uploading a tutorial or recipe that hasn't been tested and doesn't actually work. It may be uploading a review of something they haven't actually tried so the review doesn't hold true.

It's really important to come into the world of blogging with integrity. People can see through gimmicky, spammy behaviour and do not appreciate having their time wasted with low quality content. This is a surefire, guaranteed way to earn a terrible reputation and drive readers AWAY from you.

Common mindset barriers for those who want to start blogging

Let's spend some time breaking down some specific mindset barriers that prevent many people from stepping into the blogging world or giving it their all.

'I'm not a tech-savvy person, I won't be able to start a blog'

Have you ever typed out a body of text onto Microsoft Word or any similar platform?
Have you ever attached a file to an email?
Have you ever used a photo-editing app?

If you can do all these things, then I can confirm that you are indeed tech-savvy enough to start a blog.

Sure, it'll be a learning curve. In my experience, it's usually the first few days to a week which can feel frustrating, as you set up the layout of your blog and figure out the various features on WordPress.

I myself do not have ANY kind of formal training in website design or tech. Heck, I would describe myself as a 'non-tech-savvy' person to the surprise of many, despite having years of experience running multiple of my own online blogs and businesses.

If you feel overwhelmed just by the thought of the technicalities, let me share some advice with you:

1. It's not as hard as it seems, as with a lot of things. After helping several people set up their own blogs and setting up multiple of my own, trust me that this part of blogging is nothing to be worried about.

2. Most of the things you need to do to set up a blog are things you only need to do once. When your blog and layout is set up, the only things you'll need to be doing are logging into your WordPress and crafting your posts.

3. If you ever get stuck and need answers, there are a wealth of articles, forums and YouTube videos out there by people just like you, who had the exact same problem as you, who have shared the solution online. This wealth of knowledge only keeps growing as time passes - the problem you'll be having is not unique and there is always a solution available if you search for it.

4. If you choose a good hosting provider (I'll cover this in chapter 8), they will help you with any technical issues,

major or minor, you are finding difficult to navigate. Many hosting providers have an online live chat or email facility which allows you to speak to an expert and get an answer fast.

Reframing this mindset: *Technical things are not hard, they are just new to me. Others have learnt and I can learn too.*

'I'm scared I won't stand out'

We ALL have knowledge, skills and expertise in a subject that is unique. We all have something within us that someone else is seeking out.

We may have been led to believe otherwise throughout our lives. It can be a scary thought to put yourself out there and not be noticed and not be appreciated for our efforts. Sometimes this fear of rejection and being ignored can be great enough to stop us from pursuing great goals and achievements.

That's why I really emphasise the importance of good strategy and research. It's one thing having something valuable to offer to the world, and it's a completely different thing to be able to present your value in a way that actually reaches your target audience AND then resonates with them. This is also why I emphasise the importance of selecting your niche well, as standing out is definitely easier when you're competing against less of a crowd.

So in response to this fear, standing out in the busy world of blogging is not something that will come without effort. You cannot publish post upon post without thought, direction and strategy, and shout into the interwebs, 'PLEASE NOTICE ME' and expect it to work.

But don't worry about how you're going to do that for now - I will venture into that later on.

Reframing this mindset: *I have value to give to my readers and to my industry and I will learn how to best present this information and reach them.*

There are so many people doing this, I don't think there's room for me

'The best time to plant a tree was twenty years ago. The second best time is now.'

Sure, the blogging market was less saturated 5-10 years ago. That doesn't mean there isn't room for anyone new. Everyone comes with their own perspective, their own style and their own voice.

If you're worried that your ideas have already been 'taken' or 'done' and no one will be interested in you, always remember that if content like the type you want to create already exists, that is proof there is demand for it.

The fear of there not being enough to go around is rooted in a scarcity mindset - that there are finite resources, that everyone has taken what is already out there and there's nothing left for me. This quite simply is not true.

Think of it this way: imagine your friend, an exceptionally talented and knowledgeable friend, tells you they want to start a beauty salon, but they are scared because there's already one other successful salon in town. What would you tell them? Firstly, you'd probably be baffled at her logic! But then you'd move on to explaining to your friend that there is a market and room for more than one beauty salon in town, it's an evergreen service that is always needed and that if she runs her salon properly, she will do well too.

Reframing this mindset: *There's room for everyone at the table - there IS in fact enough to go around. There is an abundance of traffic, interest, readership and money to go around, and I am brave enough to tap into it.*

This mindset is POWERFUL in transforming the way you think about not just blogging, but anything you receive in life. There IS enough to go around.

'It's going to take too long - I need money now, not in 12-18 months time'

I hear you. In the era of TikToks, reels going viral and thousands of online 'gurus' talking about get-rich-quick schemes, a venture which says from the onset that it will take months before it will replace your 9-5 is not immediately appealing.

Thinking 'this is going to take too long' is a mindframe that comes from a scarcity mindset which says that I do not have the patience or time to wait for money because I need it now, therefore I am not willing to work on this long-term project that will bring me goodness in the future.

Immediate gratification is never a good, profitable business strategy. Good things take time. Here's the truth - get-quick-rich schemes are usually unsustainable, risky and unreliable.

In 12-18 months time, you're still going to be here whether or not you create a blog. The difference is if you execute your plan well, you will realistically be able to bring in some income by the 12-18 month mark which will become PASSIVE. I'm going to bring in the fruit tree analogy again - once you've planted and watered your blog plant, you will reap its fruit if you just wait.

The 12-18 month mark is just a ballpark figure. There are many ways you can accelerate this timeline. If you begin to make affiliate sales or if you create and sell a product, you could begin to make money as soon as people begin to visit your website. Supplementing your strategy with social media traffic can do wonders too. If you have a very strong strategy and are razor sharp in your focus, uploading posts regularly and are in a great niche, it could very well take less than 12-18 months to begin making money.

Reframing this mindset: I *am willing to be patient and invest in my future. Good things take time and I am in no rush.*

'I don't have a lot of money to invest into web design, photography equipment and other services'

I hear you loud and clear! Most of us do NOT have hundreds and thousands to invest in a business or a side hustle that isn't going to be bringing in money immediately.

People will TRY to tell you that in order to be successful, you need to invest in your web design, into fancy equipment and plugins and services that, quite frankly, YOU DO NOT NEED. In fact, some of these people will be trying to sell you THEIR services, which is why it's in their best interests to make you believe you need to buy something!

For the first 4-5 years of my food blog, I only paid the monthly domain fee for my blog and the yearly domain name. **On average, this cost me around £15/month**. I didn't have any fancy props or equipment. I took photos from my iPhone and I purchased a WordPress theme on Etsy for around $30 which I ran on my blog for 3 years. I did all my keyword research through free online tools and guess what? It was enough to grow my blog into a full-time business that began to make me more income than my old teaching job.

Now as a professional blogger, the monthly running expenses of my blog are no more than £75/month. For a business that makes me a full-time income even if I don't work a single hour, I'm pretty happy with that.

People often fall into the rabbit hole of believing you need all the trimmings if you want to pursue anything website-related - an all-or-nothing mentality. This is false, particularly for blogging. If you focus on creating quality content that provides your reader with what they're looking for and more, this will always be the best strategy. And anytime you feel like you're going down the rabbit hole again, remind yourself that you can invest in those things later when your blog begins to make money.

Reframing this mindset: *I don't need a lot of money to get started. I can still offer value to my readers without spending more than I can afford.*

'I won't make good money from this'

Let's break this down. Why do you think you won't make good money from it?

Perhaps you think you won't ever grow your blog enough to be able to make money from it.

Perhaps you think there's not enough room for you, and that there are already so many blogs out there making money, so there's not enough to go around.

Perhaps you think the blogging industry quite simply does not have that kind of potential for people like you.

All these thoughts are deeply rooted in the scarcity mindset. I'm here to tell you blogging is a viable way of making money and that's exactly what I'm here to teach you in this book.

Reframing this mindset: *Blogging has made hundreds of thousands of other people money and it will make me money too. There is enough to go around, there is room for me and I am ready for it.*

What I create won't be perfect enough to be online

Many moons ago, I was a newbie food blogger, armed with my iPhone 3GS taking blurry, unedited process photos in my worse-for-wear kitchen and food pictures under the harsh yellow lighting of my tubelight at 11pm.

I KNEW these pictures were not good, I knew they were not on parr with the level of photographic perfection of other food bloggers. But you know what? I also knew something was better than nothing. **Showing up with what you have is better than not showing up at all.** I am grateful I didn't listen to that inner critic inside of me that told me I shouldn't bother, because my blog grew even with those less-than-stellar pictures.

Hear me out. I don't recommend ANYONE to actively half-ass any of their work. In order to be blogging about a certain topic, you need to have a high standard of content in today's market. A 3/10 level effort just won't cut it - it won't be favoured by the search engine gods and people won't be enticed to come back to you even if they do stumble across you.

However, if you're scared about your work being an 8/10 and not a 10/10, then please do not let your fears inhibit you. Perfection is the enemy of progress. If 2015-Fatima didn't upload those blurry, dimly lit, not very aesthetic food pictures to her blog, she would have never become 2023-Fatima who is now writing a book about how her cute little blog adventures changed her life. I did the best I could at the time with the knowledge and resources available to me - and it <u>was</u> good enough.

Reframing this mindset: *It doesn't have to be perfect to help someone. It doesn't have to be perfect to provide value to my readers. And it doesn't have to be perfect to grow into something big.*

I don't want to show my face or have my privacy compromised

If this is your concern, you'll be pleased to hear that showing your face is not a prerequisite to blogging. You have complete power over what you show or don't show online. Having an online presence doesn't mean you have to lay everything out there for the world to see.

When I initially started blogging, I did have my face on the 'About Me' page of my food blog, but then removed it a few months later once I realised I didn't want my face plastered on the internet yet. In fact, I still don't have a picture of myself on any of my blogs. No one has ever made a comment about it.

The majority of readers will come to your blog, take the information they need and then leave, only to come to you again when they need more information. They aren't primarily concerned with your face, they're concerned with the information and value you're providing.

I will caveat this by saying that, generally speaking, readers LOVE seeing a face and connecting with people through visuals. It helps foster a more personal connection, helps reader retention and builds a sense of trust.

But if showing your face is a hard no and is the do-or-die decision for starting, then honestly, don't give it a second thought. Start. You don't need a picture of yourself.

Reframing this mindset: *I don't need to compromise on my privacy in order to be successful; I can find ways around it.*

I don't want to be on social media

Social media is also NOT prerequisite to starting a blog! This may be shocking advice (and maybe even borderline controversial in today's day and age), especially in a time when it feels like social media is taking over everything.

If you have a solid strategy which prioritises search engine optimisation and creating quality blog content, you do NOT need to have a large social media presence (or any at all!) to run a successful, income-generating blog. For me personally, social media brings in less than 6-9% of the total traffic on my food blog. In fact, if I was to stop posting and delete my social media apps, there would hardly be a dent in my earnings.

Does social media help at all? Yes, it does! I talk more about leveraging the power of social media further on in the book, but it is not without its drawbacks. Being on or off social media is your own choice and should you choose not to be on it, you can very easily do other things with the time you'll be saving that will grow your blog and readership.

Reframing this mindset: *I don't need to wear myself thin on social media to be successful, I can choose what I focus on and how much I focus on it, depending on my capacities.*

Positive affirmations for blogging

Okay, so I know this whole positive affirmations thing is having a bit of a moment and may feel a bit cliché or abstract to you. However, people who are successful are this way once they have mastered their inner voice. Positive affirmations, good thoughts, brain reframing - you can call it whatever you like - do really help with rewiring the way you think and this is the first step on the path to long-term success.

Take what you need from this list and remember - our greatest battles are within our own mind.

What I bring to the table is unique and valuable.

There is enough room at the table for me.

Doing something for the long term is good for me.

Time will pass whether I do something or not, so I choose to build.

I have much to gain from blogging and little to lose.

I am not afraid of failing.

I'm not afraid of hard work.

If something goes wrong, I can fix it and learn from it.

I am an expert in what I am passionate about.

I don't have to be perfect to be good enough.

It isn't hard, it's new and once I learn it, I will excel at it.

SUMMARY

Anything new can evoke feelings of anxiety, fear and dread, and starting a blog is no different. Feeling like you won't get anywhere, that there's no space for you online or that it is too hard to try, all originate from a scarcity mindset. These thoughts trap us into thinking there's not enough out there for us and if there is, we are not good enough for it. Before starting any new venture, it is key to enter with a clear mind and an abundance mindset, being open and ready to take on new challenges and believing that you will achieve what you set out to. Placing a ceiling above your head only limits you - removing that ceiling is the key to growth and success.

5

Research (1): Finding Your Ideal Reader

Identifying your ideal reader

When I started my food blog in 2015, I was only vaguely informed about the best practices of my successful peers, but the one thing I do remember doing is sitting down and writing a profile of my ideal reader.

Why does this matter? Why can't my blog suit anyone and everyone?
Because NO blog can or should suit anyone and everyone!

Every blog, every business and every institution has an ideal client or reader they are targeting their work towards. Identifying your ideal reader will help inform your decisions about: how you should be branding your blog, what type of content you should write, what sort of tone and language you should adopt in your writing, what vibe your photos should present, etc., in order to attract those ideal clients to your work.

When I wrote my ideal reader profile in 2015, it was pivotal in helping me realise that my work should NOT be written with the aim of suiting the masses, because then I would be unable to specifically attract my ideal reader. My ideal reader resonates with my writing and work. My ideal reader loves my outlook and vibe. They are a loyal reader, a fan, and will consistently return to read my new content, tell others about me, and purchase products from me down the line. Why would my ideal reader do all this? Because they know, like and trust me. **My work, my words and my brand connect with them. And you won't be able to build that connection if you are not creating your content to align with that person.**

Task: Let's begin to think about the kind of reader you would love to write for. Who is your ideal reader? Where do they live, how old are they, what sort of lives do they live, what kind of job do they have?

Then, let's dive deeper. What sort of personality do they have? What are their wishes, their dreams, their fears? What problems do they face? What are they good at?

All of these questions will lead to the formation of your ideal reader. When you begin to brand yourself and your blog, or whenever you write any content for your blog or social media, keep this ideal reader profile firmly in mind.

Branding to connect with your ideal reader

The work you do on your ideal reader profile will inform the way you brand your blog.

Branding is not just your logo. Branding is the personality you exude, the voice you use, the language in which you communicate. Branding is about SO MUCH MORE than what colours you use and how pretty your logo is - it's about how you make people *feel*.

Ask yourself questions, such as:

- What sort of vibe would look attractive to my ideal reader? Would they prefer something sleek and clear cut, or perhaps a more colourful, cheerful vibe?

- What colours represent my ideal reader? What colours can I use to appeal to the personality of my ideal reader? You may want to consider exploring the concept of colour psychology to help you decide this.

- What sort of language should I be using to make my work attractive to my ideal reader? What sort of vocabulary, tone, and voice?

- How should my photos look? Do they need to be highly professional, or can something more rough and authentic work well too?

- How should I best interact with my ideal reader outside of my blog (if I will be)? What social media networks would my ideal reader be using, if any? (Note, an interaction isn't necessarily a personal one; posting content for readers to consume is also an interaction.)

Another significant decision you'll be making when branding is what to name your blog. Your blog name should have some reflection of your niche. For example, if you have a cooking blog, the name should reflect that. Additionally, consider whether you may in the future want to move your blog in a different direction or broaden your niche and whether your chosen domain name would allow that. For instance, don't add a location if you may move towns/countries in the future, or use words such as 'mum', 'wife', 'dad' if your blog has a chance of shifting from those identities - this is a branding nightmare best avoided.

Use all this information and proceed to craft a name for your blog, a logo and create a colour palette you will be using for your layout and graphics. You could create this yourself or hire someone to do this for you if you are so inclined. When you go on to write your content, post on social media and email your readers, keep your branding in mind.

SUMMARY

Your blog shouldn't attract anyone and everyone - in order to succeed and thrive, it needs to attract a certain kind of reader; your ideal reader. How you brand yourself and your blog will then be guided by what your ideal reader will be most drawn to.

6

Research (2): Finding Your Niche

Niche: (noun) denoting products, services, or interests that appeal to a small, specialised section of the population.

Every successful book, website, blog will get one thing right: they define and OWN their niche really well.

Have you ever heard of the phrase 'jack of all trades, master of none'? Well, that sort of approach isn't going to work in the world of blogging. The best approach will always be to have a defined niche that allows you to provide a tailored and therefore enriched experience to your audience.

Most of us usually come into blogging with a rough idea of the broad niche we'd like to sink our teeth into. Maybe you're an avid gardener and want to share all your knowledge and expertise. Or a knitter who has an array of expertise, skills and patterns in your repertoire. Usually, the passion or knowledge precedes the desire to start a blog. And like I mentioned earlier, being passionate or at least knowledgeable in an area is a non-negotiable for blogging.

Here are some broad examples of niches:

- Food
- Education
- Business
- Money
- Travel
- Home
- Lifestyle
- Health
- Beauty
- Parenting

Think about one of your favourite blogs. It's highly likely you'll find that they have a well defined niche, as opposed to doing a little bit of this and a little bit of that.

That's the sort of approach you should aspire to rather than trying to write about too many topics at once.

If you do focus on a very specific niche but want to occasionally broaden out further, always remember to stay within your overall niche. For example, if you have a food blog that shares Greek recipes, it is fine to occasionally share a

Turkish recipe whilst still remaining a predominantly Greek food blog. However, it probably wouldn't be great to sporadically upload a post about investing in US real estate. No one is coming to a food blog to look for real estate advice. If you have a vast amount of knowledge about another topic, you can consider starting a second blog for it! But never combine two separate niches into one blog.

Hyperniche has been added to the conversation

So now that you've decided a broad niche for your blog, I'm going to let you in on a little secret that, if done correctly, has the ability to solidify you as an authority in your niche quicker and with better results.

Make your niche more specific. A hyperniche, if you will. Writing about a broad niche is difficult for many reasons:

- Because it is so broad, you will have difficulty establishing yourself as an expert in your niche due to the sheer quantity of posts you'd have to create, unless you dedicate all the time in the world to writing, spend years writing or hire content writers to write for you.

- You'll be up against many big organisations and websites, and trying to rank against them will be difficult.
- It can be plain overwhelming trying to zoom in and do justice to such a vast topic. Overwhelm is not your friend!

You may have thought that aiming to attract as many readers as possible by appealing to everyone is the best approach. I cannot stress this enough: that is a risky strategy.

Think of it like this: you're setting up a cake stall at a cake fair in Central London. Sure, there'll be a lot of people who want to buy some cake, but this is a CAKE FAIR IN CENTRAL LONDON. There are 100 other stalls. Competition is fierce. You need to stand out from the crowd to get noticed. You may be able to make a good day's sale, but you have to break an arm and leg attracting customers to your specific stall, marketing before the day and on the day, baking a huge variety of cakes to pique their interest, and essentially exhaust yourself because there's just too much background noise. It's a hard life.

Choosing a more specific niche is different. Imagine the following month you set up another cake stall in a smaller town in an obscure part of the country, but this time at a general food fair where there are only two other cake stalls. There's a lot less competition. The fair isn't quite so stressful anymore because you don't feel like you're up against the world. **You sell more cakes than the first fair even though this fair had fewer people coming in** and you didn't even have to break an arm OR a leg. Life is good and revenue is at an all-time high.

This is the magic of the hyperniche.

Here are some examples of hyperniches underneath the broader niches I mentioned above:

- **Food** - focusing on a specific region in the world or a dietary requirement, e.g. gluten-free recipes, Polish recipes, recipes on a budget, air-fryer recipes, Instant Pot recipes, etc.
- **Education** - can be split into educational age, e.g., pre-school, primary school, high school, University; or subject, such as a blog for nurses, doctors, teachers, estate agents; or educational approach, e.g., homeschooling, unschooling, Montessori education, Waldorf education, and so on.

- **Business** - focusing on how to start a very specific business, or zooming in certain aspects of a business, such as social media for business, customer services, etc.

- **Money** - real estate, stock investing, saving money on bills and/or groceries, best deals for xyz, etc.

- **Travel** - can be focused on travel in a specific continent or country, travelling to certain destinations, e.g. beach destinations, amusement park destinations, etc.

- **Home** - home decor on a budget, home decor in small spaces, maximalism, home decor for rentals, DIY home projects, IKEA hacks, etc.

- **Lifestyle** - low/zero waste lifestyle, vegan, religious lifestyle, etc.

- **Health** - living with specific health conditions or illnesses, particular exercise regimes, specific diets such as vegan or anti-inflammatory (many of these diet-related hyperniches are also very saturated so some further niching down would work well too), etc.

- **Beauty** - vegan and cruelty-free make-up and skincare, make-up for people of colour, zooming in on specific make-up or skincare items, like lipsticks, foundation, etc.

- **Parenting** - focusing on specific parenting approaches , parenting a certain age-group, or parenting children with specific conditions,illnesses or neurodiversity, etc.

Getting very specific with your niche may be difficult if you have many areas you feel like you could write about. It is also important to be wary of niching down too much - if you become extremely niche you could struggle to find readers. There's a sweet spot between finding a hyperniche that is specific enough for you to stand out, but not so niche that you are unable to find an audience. I'll cover how to determine this further on.

Task if you're struggling to figure out a hyperniche: Jot down a list of blog post titles you think you have the knowledge or passion to write about right now. Don't worry about hyperniches, just write down whatever comes to mind. Don't worry about anything you haven't perfected yet - just write down any posts that you have the potential to write. Keep going with this list for about 10 minutes, or until your brain goes blank - whichever comes first.

Once you're done, take a look at the list? Is there an emerging theme? …a hyperniche revealing itself?

How to assess your niche's potential

Researching is going to become an integral part of your role as a blogger. At every stage of the journey, whether it's before you start your blog or deciding what blog posts to write, research is an essential part of blogging for success. Before you dive into purchasing your blog and investing any time or resources into it, it's worthwhile assessing:

a. **Is there a demand for your niche?**

b. **How much competition is there for it?**

The following are a few relevant terms I'm going to be using in the upcoming sections which will become essentials in your blogger vocabulary.

Search volume: how often your niche is searched for on search engines such as Google. A high search volume indicates there are many people who are interested in your niche and actively searching for it. A low search volume indicates there are not many people searching your niche. **A good sweet spot for search volume is 100-1000 searches a month.**

Competition: how many other websites and bloggers are in the same niche as you, writing about the same things you want to write about, competing for the same sort of reader you are?

Low competition means there are few other websites in your niche, and high competition means you are up against many websites.

How to research your niche

The best way to conduct research into your niche is to use keyword research tools. You will need to input keywords and questions related to your niche into these research tools and they will provide you information about the search volume, competition and additional relevant metrics.

There are various free and paid tools you can use to conduct research into your niche, including:

- **Keysearch.co** (5 free searches daily in the free one month trial, then plans starting from $17/month for unlimited searches including YouTube research. **(I've shared a code for 20% off your plan at the end of the book).**
- **Wordtracker.com** (10 free searches a day, otherwise plans starting from $27/month for 1000 searches a day).
- **Ubersuggest** (3 free searches a day, otherwise plans starting from £27/month).

- **RankIQ** (no free searches, plans starting from $49/month).

- **Ahrefs** (some free tools including a keyword generator, plans starting from £79/month).

- **Moz** (10 free searches a month with a free account, plans starting from $99/month).

- **Semrush** (10 free searches a day, plans starting from $119.95/month).

(Prices displayed are exactly as listed on the respective websites, as of April 2023.)

Do you need to purchase a premium, paid keyword research tool?

Not necessarily. It certainly does help save time and resources and give you a sense of direction. However, if you're starting off, you likely won't need that level of detail and can fare well with the free searches many of the above options provide. I use the paid version of keysearch.co and I find it provides me with ALL the information I could possibly ever need without a huge price tag.

Other places you can research include:

- Facebook groups with a few hundred/thousand members.

- Amazon for books and products.
- Instagram for hashtags and accounts.
- Pinterest.
- YouTube channels with a few thousand subscribers.

You'll also need to assess how much competition there is in your niche.

You'll be able to gauge competition by performing a few Google searches about your chosen niche. A good question to ask is: how many bloggers are out there creating high quality, helpful content in your desired niche? There is a never ending sea of blogs, but you want to assess how many genuinely well-written, regularly updated and good quality blogs are in your market. Using the keyword research tools I mentioned earlier, competition is often calculated by giving a score labelled either 'competition' or 'difficulty'.

Competition shouldn't put you off, but if there is a very high amount of competition from established bloggers writing excellent content, it may be a sign that you should make your niche more specific (for example, instead of just food recipes, niche further into regional or diet-specific recipes).

Here is a table to help you consider the various situations:

	Low search volume (100 and below monthly searches)	High search volume (1000+ monthly searches)
Low competition	May indicate there simply isn't enough demand for this niche. I'd advise making your niche broader. However, I would also consider whether there are reasons to believe your market is 'up and coming' and may become more popular a few years down the line, thus making it worth the effort now. Further on in chapter 11, I discuss how low competition, low search volume niches are more likely to convert into customers for your products, which is a factor worth considering too.	Blogger's jackpot - congratulations! You're competing against very few other bloggers for a niche that people are actively searching about! If you write good quality content and run with a good strategy, there's a lot of potential for success.
High competition	Dangerous zone - definitely worth reassessing if this niche is viable for you. I'd advise shifting the direction to a broader niche and doing some research to see whether it impacts search volume and competition.	May be difficult to stand out - could potentially take more time and effort. I'd advise considering shifting down to a more specific niche to reduce the competition.

Example of niche research

This can be a bit challenging and the very concept may even be whooshing over your head right now. Let's work through an example together.

Let's say I've set out to create a blog about sewing. I've done my niche research by inputting into a keyword research tool keywords such as:

- *'Sewing for beginners'*
- *'Sewing blogs'*
- *'Sewing patterns'*
- *'How to sew'*

Using the figures and data on these keyword research tools, I can see that search volume is healthy and in the thousands, while competition/difficulty scores are moderate. This is a good indication that I may be able succeed in this niche.

I took my research a bit further and explored potential posts I could write about. Some more examples of such searches include:

- *'How to sew with velvet'*
- *'How to sew a button onto pants'*
- *'How to thread a sewing machine needle'*
- *'How to tie off a stitch'*

- *'Sewing machine reviews'*

Many terms I looked at had search volume scores between 100-1000, some had even more than 1000. Competition/difficulty scores were in the easy to moderate range too.

I know from my own experience that there are plenty of Facebook groups devoted to the craft of sewing.

Based on this research, I can conclude that sewing as a niche has good potential and I can consider starting a blog about it.

TASK: Spend some time playing around on some of the keyword research tools I've recommended. Getting comfortable with digging deep into research is a huge component for success when starting a blog, so I recommend really spending some time on this. Focus on getting a feel for exploring keywords in your niche and assessing their search volume and competition. Once you feel comfortable, grab a notebook, or a spreadsheet if that's your thing, and dive into some intensive niche research, noting down keywords which have a search volume in the hundreds, or even better in the thousands, and make a note of any competition/difficulty scores. Use this research to help you compile a list of 15-20 post ideas you can begin to work on once your blog is up and running.

Competitor research

Contrary to what that might sound like, competitor research is not the same as spying on others. It may seem like blogging is just about providing readers with a service in the form of information and content, but you should see running your blog as similar to running a business. Competitor research is a key part of establishing any business.

You can do some competitor research to…

1. **Assess how much competition there is in your niche.** Are there many other websites and blogs writing about the niche you want to write about? Too much saturation in your chosen niche may be an indication of high demand for content like yours, but it could also be a sign that niching down a bit more could be beneficial.

2. **Assess the standard of your competitors' blogs.** An overall low industry standard of content quality can be a green flag for you to jump in if you know you can create content of a much sounder quality, even if the competition is high. Google favours high quality content above all. Conversely, if there's a lot of competition and generally high industry quality, you may want to take a step back and consider niching down.

3. **Assess how well these blogs are doing.** Establishing this will allow you to assess how well you could do. One of the easiest ways to tell is to see whether they run ads (you can scroll to the bottom of their website to see what ad company they're with). If these blogs run ads with Mediavine or Raptive (previously known as AdThrive), you can safely assume they are getting good traffic and are making a decent amount of money from ads (Mediavine and Raptive need blogs to be getting 50,000 sessions/100,000 pageviews a month respectively before accepting them).

4. **See what sort of content does best.** A quick look at their best performing content will give you an idea of what sort of content is the most popular amongst your target audience. Many blogs have a 'most popular posts' or 'hot right now' category.

I do not advocate stealing other people's strategy, work or ideas. That is not what competitor research is for. When doing this research, steer clear of unethical practices including copying a competitor's style, making jibes or defaming them in your content, not giving credit if you use some of their work for inspiration, or outright stealing their content. Doing any of these can result in huge problems for you, including getting in trouble with copyright laws, being blacklisted by Google and having your reputation tarnished.

SUMMARY

It's very important to pick the right niche for your blog in order to maximise your chances of success. Researching your niche involves looking at a myriad of contributing factors including:

- search volume;
- competition; and
- the quality of the competition out there.

You can assess these factors and decide whether your niche has potential to become profitable by conducting keyword research and researching on platforms such as Facebook and Etsy. Ideally, you want a niche that has a medium to high search volume and low to medium competition. If your research suggests your niche may not be the best option, consider broadening it or making it more specific.

7

Goal Setting & Strategy

This chapter is all about setting your blog up for success - the nitty gritty deep work of planning and strategising. This background work will set you up before you even publish your first post. You can work through these things at any point either before or after you set up your blog, but it is definitely not something to overlook. Getting these things right can be incredibly powerful in pushing your blog to success.

Setting your blog up for success from day one

Everything you do should start with goal setting. Regardless of whether these are related to blogging or not, setting clear, solid goals is the first step towards achieving big things.

What is it that you seek to achieve with your blog? Where do you want to see yourself in 12 months, 2 years, or 5 years? Possible goals could include:

- I want to have published 50 posts in 12 months' time.

- I want to grow my email list to 1000 subscribers by the end of the year.

- I want to have at least one stream of income from my blog within a year.

- I want to have at least one £500 month within the next 12 months.

- I want to replace my current salary with my blogging income by 2026.

- I want to write and sell an ebook by the end of next year.

I cannot stress enough the importance of setting goals. Writing them down and reminding yourself of them often is a very powerful act. It gives you a framework to work with instead of leaving you with a vague idea that you prod at, sometimes from the left, sometimes from the right, with no vision of what you're doing or working towards.

Task: Have a long, hard think about your goals for your blog. Write down a list of goals you'd like to achieve in 1, 2 and 5 years' time. Be as specific with your goals as you can get.

I find displaying my goals somewhere visible helps remind me to stay focused - you can do this too if you'd like, or alternatively you can stick them to the front of your blog planner if you have one.

How to create a blog strategy

After you've set your goal(s), we can work on your strategy. **Strategy is how we get from A to B**, A being your current position and B being your goal. Strategy is not a long, complicated multiple-page document - it can be a pretty simple bullet-point action plan but **the key is to make it realistic, doable, and be consistent in following through with it**.

I've been guilty of creating plans that burn me out or make me hate life as I know it, making it difficult to stick to. You know your capabilities and time constraints, you know what you enjoy or are good at - keep those in mind when you plan your strategy. Do not commit to something that will exhaust you, sap the life out of you or make you feel unhappy.

For example, in terms of marketing strategy, if you do not enjoy social media and prefer writing, email marketing would suit you better. On the other hand, if you enjoy creating videos and short form content, you may benefit from a strategy that focuses on video-centric content and social media platforms, such as Instagram and TikTok. Your blog posting frequency should also be in line with what you can realistically achieve. I always recommend aiming for 30-50 posts in the first year, but you can adjust this number if you feel like it is too difficult (or too easy!)

Here's an example of the strategy I used in the first year of my food blog. It was simple, actionable and achievable for me at the time, and was geared towards setting up a solid foundation for my blog:

- 1-2 posts recipes or posts weekly with process pictures.
- Focus on evergreen recipes that people will be searching for year-round, as opposed to seasonal recipes.
- Very active presence on Instagram and Pinterest.
- Actively seek out guest posts on other blogs to get my name out there.

My current food blog strategy looks very different to the one I've just shared. My strategy has grown and evolved in line with the new knowledge I now have, is informed by research and is focused less on frequent new content on the blog and more on fostering the relationship I have with my readers. I enjoyed social media a lot in the early years, but enjoy it less so now, and therefore I have reduced its priority in my strategy. It's a much more passive model than before, and it aligns with the amount of time I have to commit to blogging in my current season of life.

That's the great thing about strategy - it evolves and grows as the business grows, based on what's working and what isn't. **A good strategy never stays the same over a long period of time.** Your strategy will also evolve and adapt in accordance to what's working for you and what you're enjoying.

SUMMARY

Going into the world of blogging with clear goals and plans is very helpful in ensuring you stay on track. It sets you up for success. Additionally, spending some time thinking about your ideal reader and how you should brand your blog to appeal to them is good practice before you begin blogging.

8

Setting Up Your Blog

This happens to be the part most people just entering into the world of blogging find the scariest. In fact, it ends up being the biggest roadblock for so many - just trying to get over the tech overwhelm!

Believe me when I say, setting up your blog is truly nowhere near the hardest part of blogging and takes very little time to do. *Repeat after me: it isn't hard, it's just new.*

In this chapter I'm going to walk you through the building blocks that form your blog (your host, your domain and WordPress) and then provide you with a step-by-step walkthrough of how to get things up and running.

Free vs paid blogs - what's the difference?

A common question I get from people wanting to get started on their blog is whether they need to get onto a paid blog hosting package, or whether they can get away with a free platform such as Blogger, WordPress.com, Medium, Ghost, Wix, etc.

The answer to this isn't so simple, but if I had to answer simply I'd say: free blogs have very limited functionality and monetisation options which don't lend well to creating a thriving business. Technically, you could run a blog that makes money on a free blogging platform, but I don't recommend it UNLESS you are blogging casually, for your own recreation, or if you don't really want to grow it into an income-generator in its own right.

The long answer: I don't recommend going for a free blogging platform because the limited capacities for functionality and monetisation are just a deal-breaker for me, and anyone who wants to make good money from their blog. Some disadvantages include:

- Very limited customisation options for your blog appearance and layout.
- Limited customer support.
- Limited memory capacity (this will be a big problem as your blog content grows).
- Many free blog platforms (e.g. WordPress.com and the free Wix plan) will show ads on your blog, but you

won't make any money from them.

- Some free blogging platforms disallow ads, affiliate links or selling products on their sites (this rule varies between platforms). Free platforms that do allow ads have a significantly less pay rate than you'd get from a paid/self-hosted platform.

- You technically don't own ANYTHING and your blog can be taken down at their discretion, for e.g. if you write about something that violates their terms and conditions.

- Most free blogs will have a subdomain attached to your blog (e.g. your-blog.blogspot.com, your-blog.wixsite.com). If you're pursuing a blog as a professional venture, a subdomain doesn't give that impression to readers.

There are only a few rare exceptions in which I'd consider recommending a free blog platform, including:

- You absolutely can NOT afford the paid hosting plan for a WordPress website. There are some pretty cheap plans out there, but for discussion's sake if we consider someone to be in this position, I'd recommend starting on either Blogger or WordPress.com with the intention of eventually migrating (moving over) to a paid

WordPress self-hosted package. I recommend these two free platforms because they can be migrated without search engine ranks being negatively impacted.

- If you're only blogging to build a readership and do not ever intend on monetising your blog (especially via ads).

- If your main intent is building a following or exposure for yourself or your brand via long form content.

To summarise this section, my recommendation for 99% of cases will be to purchase a paid blogging platform package. It's useful for you to understand the reasons behind opting for a paid option before going on to set up your blog.

Choosing your host

First thing you'll be doing is purchasing where your blog will 'live' - the 'host'. This 'host' is where you will build your website and upload your posts. Hosting is usually a monthly fee.

There's hundreds, probably even thousands, of hosting providers on the internet - which one is best for you?

This isn't a decision to take fleetingly, and **I really recommend you do your own thorough research before**

deciding which host to go with. It is possible to change your host and migrate your site from one host to another, but it's a process best avoided by making a good choice from the start.

Do not be drawn into enticing, cheap offers without doing thorough research first. I've made this mistake, persuaded by the mindset of 'Well, I'm new and not making money from this yet so I should save my money!' You get what you pay for - cheaper hosting plans are often slower, customer services are poorer, and you may be tied into long contracts. I was riddled with problems including a slow website, frequent down-time, no security certificate and spam pop-ups when I ran my fashion e-commerce website between 2017-2019, thanks entirely to a cheap hosting provider I was using. It had a terrible impact on my customers' experience on my website and I also wasted so much of my time trying to fix the recurring problems. I'd advise you to read reviews online from websites such as Trustpilot and blogs who do not have any affiliate ties with the host they're talking about before making any decisions.

My personal vote is for Lyrical Host. I have been with them for 4 years now having tried a few other hosts and I have found Lyrical Host to provide the best value for my money, stellar customer service and mind blowingly vast resource library for their members. They have a 4.7 star rating on Trustpilot which is pretty solid. As always, I advise you to do your research before choosing your host, but this is what I always recommend to friends and peers who are starting their own blog. **At the end of this book I've shared a discount code for you to get 10% off their hosting plan.**

Most hosting providers will have the option to cancel and receive a full refund within the first X number of days (varying depending on the provider) if you change your mind. If the hosting provider you sign up with does not help you or provide you with satisfactory service in the first few days, you should 100% terminate your plan with them, request a refund and find another host.

Your domain name

A domain, also referred to as domain name, is the technical term for your website. This is your website's name and ends with .com, .co.uk, .net, etc. One of your first blog set-up tasks will be to purchase your chosen domain name. Purchasing your domain name will cost between £10-20 (cost will vary based on domain name and the company providing it) and then there is usually an annual fee for renewal within the range of £10-20. You'll most likely be able to purchase your domain name from the same company you've purchased your hosting plan with (and I'd recommend you do so too; it makes things A LOT easier having everything in one place).

I discussed choosing your blog name earlier in the 'Branding' section in chapter 5. Your blog name is what will ultimately also become your domain name too. Choosing your domain name is a decision you should take some time on before making. It's not a light decision to rename your blog, both from the branding perspective as well as a search engine one, so make sure you feel 100% happy with your domain name before proceeding.

Why I recommend using WordPress

Now you've purchased your hosting plan and domain, we can go into working on the platform on which you'll be building your blog. Wordpress is the most popular blogging platform and is used by most professional bloggers. WordPress has an immense amount of functionality, customisation options and is suitable not just for blogging, but for selling products too, via their WooCommerce plugin. There's a reason why the vast majority of top bloggers prefer to use WordPress - having the huge amount of customisation options that WordPress offers really does matter as and when your blog begins to grow and you start to add more features in.

Please do not confuse this for the free WordPress.com platform I discussed earlier in this chapter. It is a bit confusing, but the WordPress platform that is hosted on WordPress.com is different (and far inferior in terms of functionality) to the WordPress hosting on a paid hosting platform.

There are a number of other website building platforms such as Wix, GoDaddy and Squarespace which are also very user-friendly with their quick and easy drag-and-drop systems. However, they are limited in their functionality in comparison to WordPress. To access the full functionality, you have to upgrade to one of the more costlier plans - but if their system cannot accommodate the functions you want, you'll just have to do without it. WordPress can seem a bit tech advanced and daunting for beginners but the learning curve isn't so steep once you get stuck into it - and the pros of the functionality outweighs the cons of the learning process. Like I've mentioned before, ANYWHERE you get stuck, you are one Google search away from hundreds of forums, YouTube videos and blog tutorials that can help you solve your problem.

How to set up your blog step by step

The process of setting up your blog is very quick and simple with Lyrical Host. This is the part most people are usually most apprehensive about but it's really not such a mountain to traverse - definitely more of a molehill that likely won't take you more than an hour to complete, tops. I've set up so many of these in my years that I know it like the back of my hand now!

1. Go onto Lyrical Host's website (lyricalhost.com), navigate to the 'register' tab and then proceed to enter your details to register for a Lyrical Host account.

2. Once registered, proceed to purchasing a hosting plan (for now, the cheapest plan to host one domain, called 'Tiny', will be enough) and your chosen domain name. You will be charged immediately for the domain and first month of hosting. Remember, I have shared a code for 10% off your hosting plan at the end of the book.

3. Lyrical Host will proceed to email you instructions on how to install WordPress onto your domain. If you have trouble with this, you can contact their support team very easily by going to support>tickets>open ticket>WordPress. Lyrical Host also has a very large bank of helpful tutorials and videos which can be found

under the Resource Library tab and also under support>knowledgebase.

4. Once WordPress has been installed onto your domain, you are ready to go! You can log in to your blog by going to the WordPress login page (your-blog-name.com/wp-admin/), which will take you to your WordPress dashboard. This is the backend of your blog. You'll access it whenever you want to upload a new post, change the appearance of your blog and make any other alterations.

If you have chosen to go with another hosting provider, they should have detailed information or videos about their setup process. If you are having trouble, do not hesitate to contact them for support - this is the service you are paying for and if they do not diligently help you, that's a big red flag and a sign that you should not go ahead with them.

Plugins to install immediately

Plugins are smart bits of software that 'plug in' to your blog and give you more functionality and ease. I like to think that plugins for WordPress are like what apps are for smartphones. They do useful as heck, smart things that make the biggest world of difference with minimal stress, if at all. You can find WordPress's database of plugins by navigating to the 'plugins' section on the left-hand navigation bar on your WordPress dashboard. Here are a few plugins you should install pretty much as soon as you finish setting up your blog to make getting started as streamlined as possible:

Google Site Kit (contains Google Analytics and Google Search Console) - this is an essential traffic monitoring plugin which should be set up ASAP. You'll need to link your blog to a Google account and it will provide you with an array of valuable metrics about your audience, such as where they found your blog, what country they're from, how long they spent on your blog, etc. Having traffic data on Google Analytics is also essential for when you will eventually apply for ad networks and/or brand partnerships, so having it set up from the get-go is good practice. Google Site Kit also sets up Google Search Console for you, which is great at tracking traffic trends, detecting issues with your website, alerting you to any issues with pages showing on Google - amongst many other things.

Yoast - my absolute favourite search engine optimisation helper. There's a free and paid version but honestly, the free version has everything you'll need. It will give you excellent SEO pointers when you are writing your posts (it will appear under the box where you'll be writing your blog posts) and I highly recommend following the recommendations Yoast has to offer you.

Jetpack - provides a number of different tools that will help your site with security, speed performance and growth.

Akismet Anti-spam - as the name suggests, this plugin protects you from spam and is particularly useful for filtering out spam comments.

A recipe plugin if you have a food blog - inputting your recipes into a recipe card plugin, as opposed to typing it out directly into your post is very important in helping search engines understand your post contains a recipe. Some good recipe plugins include WP Tasty, WP Recipe Maker and Mediavine Create Cards.

Gutenburg blocks - helps add additional functionality when you're writing up your blog posts.

WooCommerce (if you'll be selling products) - this is THE essential plugin for selling products on WordPress.

You'll inevitably also discover more plugins that you find useful as time goes on. The world of plugins can feel a bit like you've just been cast into Alice in Wonderland, but be wary of falling down that rabbit hole. Too many plugins can slow down your blog and occasionally, two plugins won't get along because of coding conflicts and can cause your blog to 'crash'. If this happens, do not panic - your blog hasn't been eaten up irreversibly. You can usually fix this situation quite quickly by contacting your hosting provider and telling them what's happened. They'll fix it for you, and probably be able to tell you which plugin caused the problem too, which is helpful.

Layouts and themes

Once you've got your blog set up and ready to go, you'll likely want to dabble into how your frontend, your actual blog, looks. WordPress has a huge variety of free themes you can choose from, and there is also an ocean of various themes you can purchase for either a one-off payment or for a subscription. Some bloggers will also choose to have a web designer custom make their theme for them.

My advice for people just setting up their blog is to not spend a huge amount of time or money setting up their layout immediately. You will definitely be able to find a theme for free or a low price that will be in line with your ideal reader and branding - it may not be the perfect vision you've set your heart on, but fixating on the aesthetics before you've uploaded any content is not a good strategy just yet. This is harder said than done, but honestly at the start, not very many people will be visiting your blog. For that to start happening, you'll need an ample amount of good quality content, so **I highly advise you to focus on getting your posts up before you work on making your blog picture perfect**.

Once you have some traffic incoming, you may choose to invest in a premium-priced theme or even pay a designer to make you a custom theme. That's entirely your own call.

I personally recommend keeping the costs down initially, especially when the blog isn't generating the money to cover those costs. Remember, people are visiting your blog for your content - I can assure you they will survive if the aesthetics of the website give off plain-Jane vibes. I know, this may be borderline controversial in a world where aesthetics are sold as the be-all and end-all. But I stand by what I said - your content is more important than how attractive your blog is.

The most important components of a theme:
- It shouldn't slow your blog down. Some themes do this, so this is one to keep an eye out for. You can check your

page speed using online tools such as Google PageSpeed Insights or Pingdom.

- Has customer support available if anything goes wonky (free themes don't tend to have this).

- Is mobile responsive (most themes are, but it is good to double check this).

- Is easy to navigate. Less is definitely more and gone are the days where javascript and fancy layouts ruled. Users generally have lower attention spans now than they did many years ago, so everything needs to be as easy as possible for them to find.

- Reflects your brand and niche. Remember all that work we did earlier about our ideal reader? We need to keep that in mind when we decide our theme. If your blog is about minimalist home decor, it doesn't make sense to have an obnoxiously bright and colourful theme - there's no way on earth that would attract your ideal reader!

Should you go for a paid theme or a free one?

Free themes hold the very obvious advantage that they are... well, free. This is a huge bonus for beginner bloggers who may not want to invest so much into their blog just yet. WordPress has a huge directory of free themes to choose from, so starting out with a free theme may make more sense for some. Free themes do tend to have limited support and customisation options. Please note that any free theme you do use should be downloaded directly from WordPress and not from a third party, unverified source.

In comparison, paid themes have more customer support and features to customise. They may have more intuitive, user-friendly features such as drag-and-drop builders. Some paid themes can be very affordable (you can find themes on WordPress.com, Etsy, and Theme Isle for under £50 one-off payments). However, there are also some highly touted themes raved about by many bloggers which are costlier. For example, the Trellis theme I've been using on one of my blogs for a few years is $15.99/month and the Feast plugin, very popular amongst food bloggers, is $249/year.

Some highly recommended free themes:
- My top pick - Kadence (free version)
- Astra (free version)
- GeneratePress (free version)
- Blocksy
- Neve (free version)

Some highly recommended paid themes:

- Astra (premium version)
- Genesis
- Kadence (premium version)
- Trellis
- GeneratePress (premium version)

Should you choose to have your website built by a web designer, be prepared to spend a pretty penny - easily in the thousands of £s or $s. It's entirely your call should you decide to invest in these services - there's not a shadow of a doubt that people love spending time on a blog that looks beautiful - but be sure to consider whether it's wise to invest in premium web design services if you're not yet earning enough to cover the costs of it. There are plenty of themes you can purchase for a one-off payment which are attractive yet very inexpensive, to bridge the time over till when your blog profits will be able to cover web design services.

SUMMARY

Getting the blog up and running may feel daunting, but is relatively straightforward. In this chapter, I've broken down the steps on how to get up and running using my hosting provider of choice, Lyrical Host. Remember, if you

get stuck at any point, do not hesitate to contact your hosting provider - it's their job to provide you with guidance and help.

9

Crafting a Successful Post

Now that we've set up the frontend and things are getting all serious and blogger-y, it's finally time to pen your first post! Invigorating! This is when things begin to feel real and exciting, especially for those of us who have a genuine passion for writing!

But… blogging isn't like those creative writing sessions from GCSE English lessons. It also isn't an outlet for all your unfiltered thoughts and feelings at length.

There was a time, 7+ years ago, when you could get away with writing pretty average-quality content online and still manage to get into the search engines' good books. But today, search engine algorithms have become very sophisticated and coupled with a more saturated market, that approach just isn't going to work anymore. We need to write to impress not only our readers, but Google too.

There are a few rules when it comes to ensuring you tick all the boxes and write your blog posts well. The good news is these rules don't require you to bend over backwards and they do become second nature once you've done them a few times.

You can begin to write your first post by logging into your WordPress dashboard, using the left-hand navigation bar to go to 'Posts' and then selecting 'Add new post'.

Here are some pointers to keep in mind when you're writing that first post - and all future posts!

Tips on writing for success

Your posts should be easy to read & scannable

Blogs are not books - people are most likely reading from the small screens of their phones and in all honesty, do not have the attention span or focus to be reading difficult chunks of information. Make your content as easy to scan through as possible by:

- Using bullet points or numbered lists wherever relevant.
- Short sentences are best. This isn't the time to show off how you know how to use all your punctuation marks in one incredibly long sentence.

- Use short paragraphs to break up long bits of text - no longer than 3-4 sentences per paragraph. It's very difficult focusing on a huge paragraph on mobile.

- Make use of headers using the H1, H2 and H3 tags to break up content and make it easier for the reader to specifically find what they're looking for. As a general rule of thumb, H1 header tags are used only for the title, H2 for subheadings, H3 for sub-categories under subheadings, and so forth.

- Main points or points with special emphasis can be highlighted in bold text or underlined so they stand out.

- Use pictures to break content up and make the reader experience more interesting. It's boring scrolling through a huge chunk of content, even if it has been broken down into more manageable chunks. People love pictures!

Write as if you're writing for a toddler

Easily one of the funniest, but best pieces of writing advice I've been given. Do not assume a certain level of competence from your reader because honestly, you don't know how experienced or inexperienced they are. To do this:

- Use simple words that anyone with a simple grasp of English will understand.

- Make your writing easily readable. That is, don't throw in long sentences, just make it a simple read. The Yoast plugin will help you with your readability by providing you with a score and giving you pointers on how you can improve readability.

- Break down the concepts of your post as if they are a beginner to this area. Do not assume they are as knowledgeable as you may be - literally assume they are a toddler.

Write a comprehensive post

Go into all the details. At minimum, a blog post should be over 1000 words but 2000 is great, and posts that have 3000 words tend to do exceptionally better than shorter posts[2]. If you cannot write at least 1000 words, consider whether this post has enough meat to be its own stand-alone post. You can do research to see how you can bulk out the post and make it more meaningful and comprehensive, but remember that any additional information you add should be valuable, not fluff.

Your post should be so well-rounded and comprehensive that it answers all your readers' questions in one place. They shouldn't need to look around for more answers elsewhere. Hook them in with your stellar knowledge, so you can cement yourself as an expert in your niche in their eyes, so that if they ever have any more questions about a topic related to your niche, they think of you.

Don't use filler words to lengthen your content

Whilst I've highlighted the importance of having a comprehensive post at least 1000 words long, we also do NOT need unnecessary filler words and sentences to artificially elongate your text. This is obnoxious, annoying and actually hurts how search engines rank your posts too. You need to strike a balance between providing valuable, comprehensive information whilst also being concise and to the point. In August 2022, Google released a new Helpful Content update and detailed how it will reward and rank websites going forward. In their own words:

'Our 'helpful content' update will better surface original, helpful content made by people, for people, rather than content made primarily to gain *search engine traffic. It's part of a broad new effort to show more unique, authentic info in search results.'*

This was a very significant update as it highlighted the importance of actually sounding like a helpful human going forward, not a robot regurgitating information to elongate a post to gain traffic. I've had experience of this myself - I've gone into old posts, shortened them to make them more concise without taking away from the information they provide, and I've been pleasantly surprised to see my Google rank go up.

Link to other relevant posts

Let's say you're a blogger in the parenting niche and you're writing a post about how to manage taking the kids on holiday. Let's also say you've already written posts in the past about managing a long road trip with the kids and fun screen-free activities to do whilst travelling with the kids. All these posts are very relevant to each other and any reader reading one of them may be interested in reading about the others too. Therefore, it's a great idea to insert a link to those articles within the post. You can do this under an 'Other posts you may enjoy' header or by organically interlinking posts throughout your text as you write your post.

Use an inviting and engaging voice

Striking a balance between adding a personal, human touch to your work without turning it into a 'dear diary...' entry is the key to nailing your blogger voice. Whilst the majority of your readers are visiting your blog for answers to questions, adding short personal anecdotal stories and tidbits increases your likeability as a writer and helps you stand out from the crowd. It makes your reader see you as more than just a source of information, but as a human just like them.

I like to remember to write like how I actually talk, not like an information overloaded robot, whilst also keeping to the topic. No one likes blogs launching into a never ending ramble (we've seen other blogs do it, and I've been guilty of it in the past, too!)

Search engine optimise (SEO) your posts

SEO is such a VAST topic, ever-evolving and the knowledge-bank ever-growing. All the pointers I have listed above will help with search engine optimisation. Other ways to increase your SEO-points include:

- Making sure you've added a description to all your images.

- Ensuring your keyword is in the title.

- Targeting your keyword well by repeating it throughout - that means it should be in your title, headings, body of the post, and in the permalink (your full URL for a post).

- Go to settings>permalinks>select post name>save. This setting makes your permalinks easier for Google to process. mygreatblog.com/my-great-bread-recipe is a lot easier for Google to read than mygreatblog.com/284042.

- Follow all the pointers in Yoast before hitting that publish button, including adding a meta description (which is the snippet of text Google shows from a website in its search results).

- Create and use post categories. They make it easier for search engines (and users) to understand the structure of your content and entire category pages can also rank on search engines.

- There's also a 'tags' section you can use. Tags are simply put, just more detailed categorisation, but not to be confused as categories. For e.g., a fruit salad recipe post may have the categories 'fruit recipes' and 'salad recipes', but it may have many tags including 'apple', 'melon', 'blueberry', 'salad', 'summer', 'healthy' etc.

Using 10-20 relevant tags per post is good practice. Categories are broad, tags are more specific.

How to use images on your blog

Photos will play a huge role in your blog, but did you know images can also be search engine optimised?

Optimising your images with just these few tips will help your images rank better, particularly on places like Google Images and Pinterest:

- You should rename your image file BEFORE uploading it to WordPress. When it's on your laptop in your gallery folder, right click the icon of the image and select 'rename'. Rename it to something that identifies what it is and uses your keyword, e.g. 'floral-wooden-blocks-1' for an image of wooden blocks with a flower pattern on them.
- When you upload your images onto WordPress, you'll have 4 labels you can fill in:
  - **Alt image**: a description of the visual of your image - for example, 'a tower of wooden blocks with pictures of flowers on all the faces of the

blocks'. The alt tag is very important - it tells search engines what the image is about and also helps explain what the image is when a graphic cannot be loaded or seen by those with visual impairment. If the image does not serve a purpose and is only decorative, leave this blank.

- ○ **Title:** as the name suggests, a title for the image. This is usually displayed when someone hovers above the image. This should have your keyword in it.

- ○ **Caption**: if your image requires a caption to be present in the post, this can go here.

- ○ **Description:** a brief description of the image, again making sure your keyword is used.

- Make sure you have a featured image - currently the optimal size recommended by WordPress is 1200 x 628 pixels however the recommended size may change depending on the theme you're running on your blog. The best way to check the size you should be using is to Google the optimal featured image size for the theme you're using . If your image isn't this size, you can resize it on the WordPress media library (which is where all the media you upload onto the blog is stored).

- Images within the body of your posts should have a 4:3

or 16:9 ratio. You'll notice that odd sized images don't tend to show in the first few pages of a Google Images search - it's because Google doesn't favour them and prefers a more standard size ratio.

- If you're using a recipe card plugin or something similar, ensure you have an image inserted into it too.

- As search engine algorithms shift towards favouring good user experience and valuable, helpful content, using high quality images becomes more and more important. They don't necessarily have to be taken on a professional camera - a modern day smartphone is good enough as long as the image itself is clear.

SUMMARY

When writing a blog post, your goal should be to craft an engaging, comprehensive and easy to read piece of work that answers all your readers questions without them needing to seek help elsewhere. There are small tweaks which will help optimise your posts for search engines - these should be done diligently, as it will help people find your blog.

10
Building Traffic

So you've completed the daunting task of purchasing and setting up your domain, you've made your blog kinda cute, and you've even uploaded a few posts! But what are these chirping crickets doing here?!

How does a blog get traffic, anyway?

Let me break down the various ways a person can find you and your blog:

1. **Organic search** - traffic that comes from people searching for content on search engines such as Google, Bing, Yahoo! and so on.
2. **Social** - people coming to your blog through clicking a link they've seen on Instagram, Pinterest, Facebook, Tiktok, Twitter, etc.

3. **Referral** - traffic that comes to your blog from other websites. So if another website links to your pineapple upside down cake recipe, it's a referral.

4. **Direct** - this is a bit of a catch-all term for many different avenues, but in theory it means people who come to your website by clicking the link directly. This may be, for e.g., someone who has bookmarked your website, received it as a text or via WhatsApp.

5. **Email** - if you have an email newsletter, you may get people who click through to your website through that (but sometimes this shows up as 'referral' traffic on Google analytics).

6. **Paid search** - traffic that comes in via paid search engine ads. I won't discuss this kind of traffic because it won't be relevant to you as a new blogger.

I'm now going to go into how you can leverage the first five of these channels to get traffic!

1. Organic search traffic

I cannot stress this enough - for any serious blogger who would like to make passive income from blogging, **organic search traffic is going to be one of your biggest games**. 8.5 billion searches are made on Google EVERY SINGLE DAY - its power and potential to drive new people to your website is unparalleled. Therefore, every effort should be made to appease the search engine gods. Appeasing them has many benefits:

- Consistent, steady, predictable traffic is pretty much guaranteed once one of your posts begins showing up on the first page of a search engine's search results for the relevant search terms. If you can manage to rank in the first few positions (at the top of the page) for a high search volume keyword, you've essentially won the search engine game and you shall be rewarded with traffic, growth and credibility.

- Showing up in the search results consistently whenever your ideal audience searches about your niche builds your credibility as the expert in your industry. Let's say you blog about crocheting. If you consistently show up at or near the top of the search results every time your ideal reader searches about crochet, and you provide them with useful and relevant information, they will begin to associate you as the go-to crochet person. They will be more likely to consistently turn to you and trust the information you share.

- Unlike other traffic channels such as social media and email, search engines will continue to show you with no effort from your end once you're up there!

So here's the deal with search engine traffic. Remember that fruit tree analogy I keep speaking about? It's kind of the same deal here too.

- When you first start a new website, you will go through a rather long spell of time where the search engines will basically give you a big fat 'who dat?' and not really give your presence much notice. This can be frustrating and off-putting, but please remember that this is very normal, even if you are doing all the right things and are writing in a low competition niche.

- Between the many blogs I have worked on/with in the past, I have noticed an unmistakable shift that occurs between 12-18 months after the first post is published. Around this time (assuming you have consistently been uploading high-quality content to your blog), something shifts and search engines begin to take notice of you. Your posts will begin to rank further up on search engines and traffic will really begin to tick upwards at this stage. There does seem to be some evidence that this shift can happen earlier - I certainly would not write it off but my experience has been indicative of a shift more likely past the one year mark.

Domain authority

As it is a very hotly contested topic in the world of blogging, I did consider not mentioning domain authority in this book. But this term is so commonly used in blogs, podcasts and other resources you may come across, that I wanted to at least touch on the topic so you know what it is when you inevitably hear the term.

Domain authority or domain rank (often abbreviated as DA or DR) is a search engine ranking score developed by the SEO software, Moz. It's a metric that predicts how well a website should rank on Google, taking into account various factors that would point to a domain being an 'authority'. In 2018, John Mueller of Google indicated that Google does not use a metric like domain authority to decide how well they rank a domain. Despite this, the concept of domain authority is still very prevailing. Whether or not Google uses a metric such as this in its system, DA is still a useful metric to consider when conducting keyword and competitor research.

2. Social traffic

Social media plays a huge, powerful role in the way we consume information today. Thanks to social media, it is significantly easier to reach your ideal reader, ideal customer and/or target audience than it was 10 or so years ago. If leveraged properly, social media can help bring in a loyal, connected audience base which has potential to grow very quickly.

Popular social media platforms that can be used include:

- Instagram
- TikTok
- Facebook
- Twitter
- Pinterest
- YouTube
- Snapchat

The primary way to leverage social media to help grow your blog is to create a social media audience and an awareness of you/your blog, and then direct them to your blog. This can be through providing nuggets of valuable information or snippets to your audience and then asking them to visit your blog for the full lowdown.

Thanks to the fancy algorithms of today however, a big downside of social media is that you need to provide a consistent stream of content to stay afloat and stand out in the sea of hundreds of thousands of other accounts. I speak from experience - this can be exhausting and can eat up precious time that could be otherwise spent writing for and improving your blog. It can become difficult to prioritise building your blog over building your social media following when the daily social media buzz draws you in. A notable exception to this is Pinterest, which is used as a visual search engine of sorts by many.

Additionally, research shows that users of certain social media platforms prefer to stay on the app and don't like to click on links that take them out to another website. This therefore means getting people to successfully navigate to your blog will (according to the data) not work very well. A 'successful' call-to-action asking viewers to 'click this link' converts around 2-5% of viewers. Again, Pinterest is an exception to this, as many people are actively looking for relevant websites to click through to.

My advice with social media is to pick one platform (no more than two if you're ambitious) to start with to ensure you're not spreading yourself too thin. Then, you can leverage its power intentionally whilst ensuring you aren't spending more time than needed on it. You can consider batch-creating and scheduling content if that helps you stay focused - there are many apps and tools that can help with this, including Canva, Hootsuite and Tailwind. If you don't particularly enjoy social media but want to benefit from its power and leverage, you can consider outsourcing services once your blog begins to earn money.

Remember that **your home ground should always be your blog**. In the majority of cases, social media will NOT be your largest driver of traffic, SEO will. Therefore aim to spend more time on your blog creating & optimising your posts and establishing your authority on your blog than you do on social media.

3. Referral traffic

Referral traffic is any traffic that comes from another source, such as other websites which have linked to your posts. Google Analytics can show you exactly what sources those are. You'll be able to see what they linked to and why (such as, if another blogger is raving about your cake recipe and gave it a mention on their latest post) and this is a great opportunity for you to see what kind of content is doing well.

4. Direct traffic

Direct traffic is any traffic that arrives at your blog by directly clicking your URL or by them manually typing it into their browser. If Google cannot identify where the traffic comes from, it sometimes gets lumped into the Direct segment too.

5. Email traffic

Emails are a gold, evergreen way of connecting with your audience and retaining their readership. Reaching out, fostering a relationship with your readers and promoting yourself, your blog and/or your products via email is called email marketing.

If Google were to roll out a crazy new algorithm that took your website from the 1st page down to the 10th page (unlikely, and also every blogger's nightmare!), or if your primary social media platform was to go into administration, suspend your account or be outright banned, how would you reach your audience? This is why the importance of email cannot be underestimated. Email is the one thing that everyone uses. These days, people receive emails directly to their phones via email messaging apps which they can (and do!) check several times a day. It's intimate, personal and extremely effective.

Here's a VERY brief summary of how email marketing works:

- You sign up for an account with a mailing service. These help organise and effectively manage your email marketing strategy. I'll be recommending some providers further on.

- You then entice your readers into sharing their email with you - the most popular way is to offer them something called a 'lead magnet' (any variety of free online resources such as an ebook). In exchange for this lead magnet, your readers will provide you with their email address. Alternatively, you can just ask them to sign up to your email list for updates from you. The former is definitely more effective though.

- Now that you have their email address, you can keep in touch with your reader on your own terms. You can send emails and newsletters providing updates on new posts or redirect readers to other content on your website on a regular schedule.

- Consistently sending your readers emails that they enjoy and find valuable fosters their fondness for you. As such, they become returning readers and, if you sell products, potential customers.

To reiterate, the above is a **very** simple summary of email marketing and its uses. While it is beyond the scope of this book to go into further depth on this topic, I want to stress that email marketing is an enormously useful tool to connect with readers and it is certainly something to bear in mind and explore further when you're ready.

There are a lot of mailing services on the market. Here is a list of a few of the most popular:

- **Mailerlite** - free for up to 1000 subscribers, then plans start at $9/month.
- **ConvertKit** - 30 day free trial, then plans start at $9/month.
- **FloDesk** - monthly fee of $35 regardless of how many subscribers you have.
- **MailChimp** - Limited functionality for free for up to 1000 emails a month; for more functionality, all paid plans come with a free one month trial, then plans start at $20/month.

(Prices displayed are exactly as listed on the respective websites, as of April 2023.)

I have used a number of these providers and am now quite

satisfied with Mailerlite. I've shared a discount code that you can use for them at the end of this book.

SUMMARY

There are a variety of different ways you can grow your blog traffic, all of which are discussed in this chapter. In the long game, search engine traffic will be your biggest ally.

11

Ways To Monetise Your Blog

Here's the million dollar question. I've got the blog, I've done the work, I've got great ideas, I've learnt the SEO… now how do I make money from it?

There are four broad ways of making money from your blog - display ads, affiliate marketing, working with brands and selling products. It's always a good idea to not keep your eggs all in one basket and to diversify your streams of income, which is just a fancy way of saying you should have more than one way of making money from your blog.

Before I begin breaking down the four ways to monetise your blog, I think it is really important to be transparent and honest with you, as I have been throughout the book. I'm going to reiterate this again: in the early months, possibly even up to 18 months, you may not make a lot of money from your blog, even if you are putting out the best, well researched content consistently. You must keep in mind from the get-go that blogging is a slow-burner - it just takes time. Don't let this stop you from continuing to put out the good content. Don't hyperfixate too much on making money during the first year - your primary concern should be around the quality and quantity of your content. The money will naturally follow (and it may well begin trickling in during the first year if you play your cards right!)

1. Display ads

Display ads are the ads you see on websites and blogs - some are in the text you're reading, some are at the footer of the page, some are videos or pop-ups. Display ads are a very passive way of making income on the blog as you are paid just for having them on your blog for readers to see (or scroll past!)

How much you're paid from display ads is calculated by a metric called RPM or CPM (revenue or cost per mile), which is just a fancy way of saying you're paid per 1,000 views. RPMs/CPMs vary on a daily basis and are impacted by many factors including time of the year, holiday seasons, how well-optimised your blog is for ads, and much more. Due to this, display ad revenue will never be the same day-to-day; fluctuations are very normal.

In order to set up display ads on your blog, you will need to submit an application to ad networks to be approved.

Every ad company has their own criteria, and if they take you on, also has their own method of onboarding.

Here are some popular ad networks:

Google Adsense: no traffic requirements (so you can start up as soon as you start your blog). As the bar to entry is so low, so are the payouts - the average RPM with Google Adsense is $2-5, making it the lowest paying display ad network and it would be very difficult to make a substantial display ad income from Google Adsense alone. In order to make a meaningful amount from Google Adsense, you'd need a huge amount of traffic.

Ezoic: also has no traffic requirements, but currently you need to complete their free ad training course before they are able to onboard you. Information about Ezoic's average RPMs are muddy, there are various claims online that they can be very high, but a survey from productiveblogger.com[1] indicates it is closer to around $4-7.

SHEmedia: requires a minimum of 20,000 pageviews per month and a higher percentage of traffic from the US. Important to note, you will also sign an automatically renewing 12-month contract with SHEmedia before being onboarded, meaning you will not be able to move to another ad network unless you give notice 60 days prior to the contract renewing. This is one of the strictest termination policies I have come across. Average RPMs are within the range of $10-20.

Monumetric: requires a minimum of 10,000 pageviews per month, 50% of which should be from the US, UK, Canada or Australia, and also has a one-off set-up fee of $99 to have all the relevant coding for the ads set up on the blog (this is the only network of this list that has a set-up fee). RPMs have been quoted to be within the range of $5-20, making this a good ad network to join once your blog has started to grow.

Mediavine: requires a minimum of 50,000 sessions per month with a majority of the traffic from English-speaking countries. Mediavine, along with Raptive, have the highest average RPMs in the industry, with a ballpark figure that hovers around $15-25 depending, as discussed earlier, on a huge variety of factors including niche, quality of content and the time of year.

Raptive (previously known as AdThrive): requires a minimum of 100,000 page views per month with a majority of the traffic from English-speaking countries. Average RPMs are in a similar range to Mediavine at around $15-25, also variable depending on many factors.

Getting into the latter two display ad networks is seen as an unofficial rite of passage for many bloggers because of the significant boost in RPMs. For some, it's the pivotal point at which blogging turns from a hobby that brings in a small side income into something much more substantial and serious. Just doing the maths, a blog that gets 50,000 sessions/month, is onboarded onto Mediavine and has an average RPM of $18, will make $900/month. If the same blog grows and begins to get 120,000 sessions/month AND also makes tweaks to their blog to increase the RPM and get it to $22, they'll be making $2,640/month. From there on it's just a numbers game. More traffic = more income.

The downside of display ads?

- Too many ads, pop-ups and video ads can clutter up a blog. At best, this annoys readers slightly and at worst, drives them away. However, reducing the quantity of ads on the page brings down your RPM and therefore your income earned, so it is a bit of a delicate dance finding the right balance.
- In periods of economic decline like we've been seeing in recent times, businesses tend to spend much less of their budgets on advertising, which has a negative knock-on effect on the advertising industry. Many of

those who rely on display ads as their main or only source of revenue from blogging will have felt the pinch as their ad income will have dropped. This really highlights the importance of diversifying your streams of income, so that if one stream takes a blow, it is covered by other streams.

- Evidence suggests that having ads on the same page as a product leads to fewer sales - just something to keep in mind if you'll be selling products on your blog.

I would recommend spending some time doing research before signing up to any ad network and finding out about how their ads will impact website speed, whether you'll be tied up into any contracts, and how often you'll be getting paid. Spend time reading about other bloggers' experiences too, not just what these networks say about themselves on their own promotional pages. A quick Google search will show tens of hundreds of people sharing their experiences with each ad network including income reports and their personal views of what approach/companies worked best for them.

2. Affiliate marketing

Affiliate marketing is promoting products and receiving a small commission from the company if a product is purchased via your links or referral codes. Many companies have an affiliate programme, including Amazon, Instant Brands, TripAdviser, Shopify, Canva… the list is honestly endless. There are also affiliate networks such as AWIN which work with companies like Etsy, Ninja, and Dyson just to name three. You can apply to various companies' affiliate programmes and will be given a referral link or code which you can link on your website and/or social media pages for readers to click through to. Once a purchase is made, you are compensated with either a percentage of the sale which varies from company to company, or a fixed amount preset by the company.

Affiliate marketing can be quite lucrative as some brands can pay out very high commissions. However, affiliate marketing can also be finicky as it's essential to be organic and natural in promoting your links. Sounding like a spammy, pushy salesman is not a good idea. As always, writing good quality content that delivers value is paramount, and weaving affiliate links organically through your post will be your best bet at earning money without giving your readers the ick.

I'd like to make a mention here of the importance of honesty and transparency whilst promoting products. Promoting products which are of low quality reflects badly on you and your business. Additionally, in line with the UK's Consumer Protection from Unfair Trading Regulations 2008 (CPUTR) and the US Federal Trade Commission (FTC) you must openly disclose that the links you are sharing are affiliate links and that you are being compensated by the companies, so that your reader can make an informed decision about whether to purchase through your link or not.

3. Working with brands

Depending on the size of your readership, working with brands can also be very lucrative. Brand partnerships usually involve them sending you their product to either review or write about in exchange for payment.

Getting connected with brands may involve:
- you reaching out to them directly (usually via email) with a pitch proposing a collaboration;
- them reaching out to you (realistically only likely if you are an industry lead or visible in the niche); or,

- by placing yourself on platforms which connect brands to bloggers and influencers. There are many platforms like this, including Aspire IQ, influencer.co, Brandback, and Tapinfluence. Some of these platforms may prefer bloggers with a social media presence.

You will usually be provided with the requirements of the deal, the sort of content you are expected to produce and any deadlines. The payment amount should be decided in advance. Everything should be in writing.

There are some pros and cons to working with brands, as with everything.

Some pros include getting the chance to work with great brands that align with your niche and/or values whilst also making money from it. Payouts from sponsorships can be lucrative if you know how to negotiate well. Sometimes sponsorships can become long term partnerships too, making it a great opportunity for a consistent stream of income.

However, working with brands is not for everyone. Working on the brand's terms, with their deadlines and producing the kind of content they want removes some of the autonomy that you have creating your own content for yourself.

If you aren't good with working in this way, this may not be ideal for you. In addition to this, reaching out to brands or waiting for them to reach out to you makes it difficult to create a consistent income. And further to that, larger brands with better payouts may not be keen on working with blogs who do not have a large readership yet.

4. Selling products or services

Research shows that bloggers who include selling a product into one of their income streams earn a significant amount more than bloggers who do not - and that makes sense! Making just one sale a day which brings in a profit of £10 can lead to £3,650 extra revenue generated in the entire year - playing a bit around with the numbers can show you how just a few sales a day can really ramp up your revenue.

Physical products that tie into your niche can be a massively profitable way to make money from your blog. In fact, research from HubSpot[3] finds that online businesses that also have a blog receive 55% more traffic than businesses that don't. Woocommerce on WordPress makes selling online alongside a blog very intuitive and simple.

Below are some examples of physical products that can tie in very well with various niches:

- **Food niche:** recipe books, special blends of spices crafted by yourself, dishware or cookware, speciality food items.
- **Education niche:** children's worksheets, notebooks, stationary, journals, books.
- **Beauty:** make-up products or equipment, beauty accessories, make-up bags.
- **Home:** decor items such as framed art, display pieces, placemats, coasters.
- **Travel:** luggage bags, passport holders, maps, travel journals.

The list is truly endless!

Digital products include ebooks, printable resources, online courses, webinars, masterclasses and workshops. These have been gaining a huge amount of traction over the last few years. In fact, the digital product market is growing twice as fast as the physical goods market - it is estimated that $54 million was globally spent on digital products in 2022 and this is expected to grow to $74 million by 2025[4]. The great thing about digital products is they can be a very passive way to earn income once they are up and running compared to physical products, which involve the whole process of sourcing, storing, packaging, and posting.

Both physical and digital products can be sold on Wordpress's Woocommerce plugin, or integrations can be made easily with Shopify, Payhip, Etsy, and Amazon.

At this point, it feels highly relevant to mention the potential for revenue from YouTube too if you'll be diving into video content. I haven't given this its own section since technically YouTube is a separate entity to a blog, but they complement each other very well. YouTube has great income-generating potential in its own right, and it would be unfortunate to not take advantage of it if you'll be creating video content for your blog.

Task: We have a lot to unpack in this chapter! Since most people's ultimate goal with a blog will be to eventually earn an income from it, it makes sense to have an action plan for monetisation.

Let's think about the four avenues of monetisation we've discussed and how you want to go about monetising your blog.

Affiliate marketing

List a few products that tie in well with your niche, that you could promote on your blog. If you can, go one step further and write down possible post ideas that would tie in organically with these products:

Working with brands

List some brands that tie in with your niche that you'd be keen to work with. If you can, go one step further and write down some post ideas that would tie in with these brands:

Selling products

Have a think about whether you'd eventually be willing to branch your blog out into a business selling products. If you're open to the idea, what sort of products could sell? How about pricing, what sort of a range would you aim for? Think about physical and digital products too. If you feel stuck, now's a good time to research the market out there:

SUMMARY

There are multiple potential ways you can make money from your blog. Display ads, affiliate links and selling digital products are the most passive methods but require an audience in order to make a sizable amount of income. In fact, display ads and affiliate marketing can become very lucrative along with being passive in nature if there is a lot of incoming traffic. Working with brands and selling a physical product are also options to monetise your blog without necessarily needing a large audience (although a large audience always helps!)

12

Next Steps: Blogging & Beyond

So you've gotten your blog up and running, it's looking good and you've even published a few posts which you've crafted using all the tips and tricks in this book. Congratulations!

I wrote this book as a starting point for people who want to get into blogging but needed that 'how, what, why' boost. Once you've started and know the basics, blogging is pretty much a rinse-and-repeat cycle of researching, creating and uploading new content.

But… What now? Where do you go from here?

Here is some advice, from this veteran blogger, on how to keep on your A-game whilst on this journey.

Strategise and remain consistent

I cannot stress enough the importance of remaining consistent. I fell into this trap when I abandoned my food blog in 2017-2018, albeit due to circumstances out of my control, and it cost me thousands of pounds and so many potential opportunities. Don't forget, 'strategy' is not a scary, business insider word, it just means a plan of how you're going to get from A to B. Go through the book, decide what kind of strategy will work best for you and stick with it for a few months. Then go in, assess how it's working, revise it if needed and keep at it. Remember the fruit trees, my friends.

Fit blogging into your routine

I hear you, it's hard fitting something into your day when you're busy working and it doesn't bring any money yet. The keyword here is YET.

I always remind those around me who are starting off with a new blog (and sometimes I need this reminder too) that the price of entry to a whole potential world of income and success is this time you put in. It's an investment into the future-you. Once you break into income-earning territory, you'll see that fruit tree.

My advice when trying to fit in blogging with a busy schedule is to first carve out solid time during the first 1-2 weeks dedicated to the initial set up, figuring out the WordPress system and then cranking out some of those first posts. When you start something new, you'll be on a bit of a natural dopamine high so let's capitalise on that by setting aside time for some deep, focused work!

Once the dopamine settles down, you'll need to find some regular time in your week to dedicate to your blog. This will look different for everyone, whether that be early mornings or evenings or maybe even just weekends, but the key is to identify that ideal time and then to stick with it consistently, instead of thinking 'I'll work on it whenever I have some free time'. You know what happens when you say that? You never find free time. Because there's always something to do, somewhere to go, someone to meet. Blogging will slip down in priority because it isn't urgent enough. The solution is to schedule it into your routine and stick with it.

Learning and improving your craft is a never ending process. Prioritise it.

Blogging is an ever evolving field with so much to learn about. This book is just the start of your journey and you will continue to learn so much as you progress and grow your content. Keep in the loop of new updates, good practices and SEO tips by reading other blogs, listening to podcasts and consuming high-quality blogging-related content. Education is a forever process - I'm inclined to say it's one of the most important components to growing in this industry. In order to be successful and stand out in your industry, you have to carve some time out to keep learning. This learning doesn't specifically have to be about blogging, it can also be about ways to improve your mindset, productivity, writing skills, work/life balance, and so on.

Monitor performance and trends with Google Analytics and Google Search Console

Keeping an eye on how your blog is doing is a must. You should monitor your posts to understand what is working and what isn't. Google Analytics and Search Console are both invaluable tools that will help you identify where you are most successful, any emerging trends, and which parts of your blog need tweaking. Search Console will also alert you to any issues on your website such as poor loading speed, so it is very much worth keepings tabs on.

Don't forget old posts! Continue to optimise and update them even after they're published

With my current two established blogs which have their foundations laid down, I find that I spend a lot more time going back to optimise and improve older posts than actually creating new ones. It is good practice to intermittently go back into posts to add more detail or relevant information, provide updates if things have changed about a topic, reformat where appropriate, and add some more SEO magic that you've learnt.

If your ranking for a particular post on Google drops (something you should be keeping an eye out on Google Search Console and/or Analytics), then going into that post to freshen things up and add more value can be pivotal in getting your rank back up.

Join blogger communities

Running a blog can be a lonely business - I speak from experience. For a very long time, no one I knew had any kind of interest in the blog industry, so I was very much out of the loop if anything new happened, nor did I have anyone to bounce my ideas off. Joining a few blogger Facebook groups really bridged this gap for me. All of a sudden, I was aware of algorithm changes, new trends and finally felt connected to the blogger community at large. Surrounding yourself with likeminded people who share similar goals to you makes a big difference! You will find a variety of groups on places such as Facebook, reddit and even Twitter.

Keep an eye on Google algorithms (they change too!)

Although in my experience these algorithms are not as volatile as social media algorithms, changes do occur and it can mean your ranking comes down (or up!) and will need your attention.

I firmly believe that if you are writing high-quality, valuable content that is search engine optimised, algorithm changes will not have a massive impact on you. At the end of the day, any changes to the algorithm will always be to enable Google to help more users find the best information. If your content is the best it can be, you don't need to lose sleep over any search engine algorithm changes. However, because it is so impactful, I still like to keep an eye out on any changes. The best place is at the heart of the source, on the Google blog (https://developers.google.com/search/blog), but most of the time I'm alerted to them via Facebook blogger communities. This isn't something you need to do very regularly, but it's something to keep in mind since it can have such a big impact on your blog.

Consider the use of videos

It is undeniable - people are moving more and more towards video content. This is something you may choose to incorporate into your strategy and use to your advantage. Video complements some niches particularly well, such as beauty, food and travel, so it's a good idea to embrace video if you can. If you are confident with this form of content, you can consider creating videos and uploading them onto YouTube for your blog readers. YouTube videos can be embedded into blog posts where relevant. Bonus: you may even be able to monetise those videos down the line once they reach YouTube's monetisation requirements.

Artificial Intelligence (AI) tools are here to stay. Learn how to use them to your advantage

I haven't mentioned AI tools at all during this book for many reasons - at the time of writing we're still in the early stages of understanding fully what the implications of it may be on the blogging industry, and overall it doesn't have an impact on the main pillars of what makes a good, successful blog.

To be honest, when the first instances of AI tools like ChatGPT producing huge amounts of coherent, informative long form text started to surface, my initial reaction was panic. What is the future of blogging and writing if robots can do it for us?!

That panic didn't last long, thankfully. A deeper look into things made me realise AI may be able to produce long-form content, but it won't be able to produce long-form content written by a thoughtful, passionate and talented human who has a long-standing connection with their readers. People come to blogs for information but turn into returning readers and fans because they resonate with you as a person. Until artificial intelligence reproduces that, I won't worry.

Having said that, as with all new advancements, it's good to embrace whatever may actually benefit you. And there's a lot of room for AI to benefit bloggers and give you an edge WITHOUT it turning all your content into lifeless robo-talk. Here are some ways you can use AI to help you with your blog without compromising on your original, authentic voice:

- Use it to help you explain more complicated concepts you're struggling to write in a concise and coherent way.
- Use it as a starting point for a blog post, then edit and weave the information together using your own style of writing.
- Use it for research and content ideas.
- For longer pieces of informative text, it can save you a massive amount of time doing research and compiling the relevant information together.
- Sometimes we get writer's block - it happens to us all! AI tools can really help in those moments by providing you with the bulk of what you want to convey, requiring

you to touch it up and piece together a post even when you don't have the brain power to do it yourself.

Topics for further reading

This book has given you an introduction into everything you'll need to start up your blog and get things running. Having said that, some of the topics I've touched on are vast and it would benefit you to spend some time doing further reading and research throughout your blogging journey. These topics include search engine optimisation which I highly recommend you doing a deep dive into, followed by familiarising yourself with email marketing and building backlinks. If you decide to have a social media presence, it would be worthwhile reading about social media marketing too.

Final Words

The book I wish was handed to me when I started my first blog in 2014 - I've just gone ahead and written it for you. 2014-me would be pretty blown away if she got to hear this is what future-me was getting up to.

I want you to really embed this in your minds and hearts: **anyone can do what they set their mind to**. Once you get over the mental roadblocks and mindset barriers holding you back, you'll find before yourself a vast plain of potential success, growth and income. Of course, that doesn't mean everyone DOES achieve what they set out to - you need to learn the right steps. And that's where this book comes in.

Blogging is very much a long-term journey. A lot of the information laid out in this book may be very new to you and you may be feeling a bit overloaded with information by the end of it (but I hope you're not!) If you are feeling this way, please remember the golden words: *It's not hard, it's just new.* You'll pick up a lot of things along the way as you put into action the things I've written about and very soon it will become second nature. You learn on the job as you potentially make some money too, kind of like an apprenticeship.

If you take anything from this book, let it be this:

Blogging has the potential to bring in an income with no glass ceiling… *only if you are brave enough to build it.*
Blogging is a viable and potentially lucrative way to bring in passive income… *only if you are willing to put in the upfront work.*
You don't need to be a tech guru or full-fledged expert to start a blog… *but you do need to be willing to learn new skills.*
It does take time, but the rewards of building something for your future is worth it.

Blogging has afforded me a life of mental freedom and the luxury of time. That is time I can now spend with my family, especially my young children who are at that fleeting young age I want to soak up and enjoy. I don't worry about childcare, school pick-ups, job deadlines or workplace anxiety. I built these foundations years ago, and now I work a few hours a week (some weeks none at all) and I know I am very comfortably covered. I would love that for you too.

I hope this book has helped you gain clarity and confidence about starting a blog. I wish you all the success in the world on your blogging journey ahead.

With love.

Fatima x

Glossary

There is a lot of vocabulary here but don't let that put you off! These are all just standard terms for very uncomplicated things - you will get used to them very soon. Please bear in mind that the definitions provided below are in reference to blogging.

Affiliate/affiliate marketing: commission made from sales generated when an individual refers/promotes an online retailer's products or services

Algorithm: a set of formulas and calculations used by a system to solve a problem. In the case of search engines and social media, an algorithm helps determine what content to prioritise, display and favour.

Backend: the controls accessed behind the scenes of the website which allow you to upload posts, tweak the layout, moderate comments, etc.

Blogging platform: the system which allows you to build a blog on a website. Blogging platforms include WordPress, Blogger, Blogspot etc.

Competition: how many other websites, blogs or people are writing about the same or similar niche as you.

Content: a piece of writing, video, audio - anything that a user can consume or take in.

Display ads: advertisements displayed through visuals such as images and videos

Frontend: what a blog or website looks like to others when it is clicked on. Your homepage, blog posts and all your blog pages are the frontend.

Google core update: when Google updates its algorithm to change how it analyses and displays search results.

Monetisation/monetise: how to make money from something.

Niche: a specific area or topic, such as parenting, food, lifestyle, travel, etc.

Permalinks: the complete URL for a specific page, post or piece of content on your site.

Plugin: a piece of software that 'plugs in' to your site, enhancing its functionality.

Search engine: websites like Google, Bing, Yahoo! etc., where people search for information.

Search engine optimisation (SEO): techniques to help a blog or website be better understood by a search engine, so that it can be shown in a high position on the results for a search query.

Search query: what someone is typing into a search engine.

Search volume: how often a term is searched by users on a search engine.

Traffic: how many people visit a blog or website.

WordPress media library: where all the media uploaded to your site (including images, videos, audio and documents) are stored and accessed.

References

1. **Article:** 'How much do bloggers REALLY earn in 2023? (Statistics from the Blogging Income Survey 2023)'
URL:
https://www.productiveblogging.com/how-much-do-bloggers-earn/

2. **Article:** 'What is the Optimal Content Length? – Here's What the Science Says'
URL: https://torquemag.io/2018/04/optimal-content-length/

3. **Article:** 'Study Shows Business Blogging Leads to 55% More Website Visitors'
URL:
https://blog.hubspot.com/blog/tabid/6307/bid/5014/study-shows-business-blogging-leads-to-55-more-website-visitors.aspx

4. Document: 'Opportunities in the metaverse'

URL:

https://www.jpmorgan.com/content/dam/jpm/treasury-servic es/documents/opportunities-in-the-metaverse.pdf

Affiliate Links

If you make a purchase using any of these links or referral codes, I make a small commission at no extra cost to you. I only recommend services I personally use and find benefit me and my blogs.

Lyrical Host - my hosting provider of choice. I currently host all of my blogs with them. I have had experience with a number of hosting providers prior to Lyrical Host and I've found Lyrical Host to be the best value for money. Their customer services are prompt and helpful and they provide members with a huge resource library full of stock images, workbooks and guides to help you become a better blogger, social media post templates, and so much more. Their 'Tiny' plan is the most appropriate plan for beginner bloggers, costing £13.99. **Use the code 'fnasim' for 10% off your plan.**

Mailerlite - my mailing service provider of choice. They provide a free plan for up to 1000 subscriber sign ups, which is plenty of capacity for a new blogger. By using the following link, you can get $20 credit when you sign up to a paid plan:

Keysearch.co - my keyword research tool of choice. It's a comprehensive tool used by professional SEO auditors and provides me with all the information I could require. The 'Starter' plan is more than enough as a beginner. Scan the following QR code and enter the code **'KSDISC'** for 20%

ABOUT THE AUTHOR

F. Nasim started blogging in 2014 and has since worked on a collection of 6 blogs and websites from a variety of different niches including food, fashion and education. She now works with others who also want to build and grow their own profitable, successful blogs.

She currently lives in Nottingham, UK, with her husband and two children.

Printed in Great Britain
by Amazon

22745251R00116